Serverless Architectures On A
Complete Self-Assessment Gu

The guidance in this Self-Assessment
On AWS best practices and standards in business process architecture,
design and quality management. The guidance is also based on the
professional judgment of the individual collaborators listed in the
Acknowledgments.

Notice of rights

**You are licensed to use the Self-Assessment contents in your
presentations and materials for internal use and customers
without asking us - we are here to help.**

Trademarks

Many of the designations used by manufacturers and sellers to
distinguish their products are claimed as trademarks. Where those
designations appear in this book, and the publisher was aware of a
trademark claim, the designations appear as requested by the owner
of the trademark. All other product names and services identified
throughout this book are used in editorial fashion only and for the
benefit of such companies with no intention of infringement of the
trademark. No such use, or the use of any trade name, is intended to
convey endorsement or other affiliation with this book.

Copyright © by The Art of Service
http://theartofservice.com
service@theartofservice.com

Table of Contents

About The Art of Service

The Art of Service, Business Process Architects since 2000, is dedicated to helping stakeholders achieve excellence.

Defining, designing, creating, and implementing a process to solve a stakeholders challenge or meet an objective is the most valuable role... In EVERY group, company, organization and department.

Unless you're talking a one-time, single-use project, there should be a process. Whether that process is managed and implemented by humans, AI, or a combination of the two, it needs to be designed by someone with a complex enough perspective to ask the right questions.

Someone capable of asking the right questions and step back and say, 'What are we really trying to accomplish here? And is there a different way to look at it?'

With The Art of Service's Standard Requirements Self-Assessments, we empower people who can do just that — whether their title is marketer, entrepreneur, manager, salesperson, consultant, Business Process Manager, executive assistant, IT Manager, CIO etc... —they are the people who rule the future. They are people who watch the process as it happens, and ask the right questions to make the process work better.

Contact us when you need any support with this Self-Assessment and any help with templates, blue-prints and examples of standard documents you might need:

http://theartofservice.com
service@theartofservice.com

Included Resources - how to access

Included with your purchase of the book is the Serverless

Architectures On AWS Self-Assessment Spreadsheet Dashboard which contains all questions and Self-Assessment areas and auto-generates insights, graphs, and project RACI planning - all with examples to get you started right away.

How? Simply send an email to
access@theartofservice.com
with this books' title in the subject to get the Serverless Architectures On AWS Self Assessment Tool right away.

You will receive the following contents with New and Updated specific criteria:

- The latest quick edition of the book in PDF

- The latest complete edition of the book in PDF, which criteria correspond to the criteria in...

- The Self-Assessment Excel Dashboard, and...

- Example pre-filled Self-Assessment Excel Dashboard to get familiar with results generation

- In-depth specific Checklists covering the topic

- Project management checklists and templates to assist with implementation

INCLUDES LIFETIME SELF ASSESSMENT UPDATES

Every self assessment comes with Lifetime Updates and Lifetime Free Updated Books. Lifetime Updates is an industry-first feature which allows you to receive verified self assessment updates, ensuring you always have the most accurate information at your fingertips.

Get it now- you will be glad you did - do it now, before you forget.

Send an email to **access@theartofservice.com** with this books' title in the subject to get the Serverless Architectures On AWS Self Assessment Tool right away.

Purpose of this Self-Assessment

This Self-Assessment has been developed to improve understanding of the requirements and elements of Serverless Architectures On AWS, based on best practices and standards in business process architecture, design and quality management.

It is designed to allow for a rapid Self-Assessment to determine how closely existing management practices and procedures correspond to the elements of the Self-Assessment.

The criteria of requirements and elements of Serverless Architectures On AWS have been rephrased in the format of a Self-Assessment questionnaire, with a seven-criterion scoring system, as explained in this document.

In this format, even with limited background knowledge of Serverless Architectures On AWS, a manager can quickly review existing operations to determine how they measure up to the standards. This in turn can serve as the starting point of a 'gap analysis' to identify management tools or system elements that might usefully be implemented in the organization to help improve overall performance.

How to use the Self-Assessment

On the following pages are a series of questions to identify to what extent your Serverless Architectures On AWS initiative is complete in comparison to the requirements set in standards.

To facilitate answering the questions, there is a space in front of each question to enter a score on a scale of '1' to '5'.

1 Strongly Disagree

2 Disagree

3 Neutral

4 Agree

5 Strongly Agree

Read the question and rate it with the following in front of mind:

'In my belief, the answer to this question is clearly defined'.

There are two ways in which you can choose to interpret this statement;
1. how aware are you that the answer to the question is clearly defined
2. for more in-depth analysis you can choose to gather evidence and confirm the answer to the question. This obviously will take more time, most Self-Assessment users opt for the first way to interpret the question and dig deeper later on based on the outcome of the overall Self-Assessment.

A score of '1' would mean that the answer is not clear at all, where a '5' would mean the answer is crystal clear and defined. Leave emtpy when the question is not applicable or you don't want to answer it, you can skip it without affecting your score. Write your score in the space provided.

After you have responded to all the appropriate statements in each section, compute your average score for that section, using the formula provided, and round to the nearest tenth. Then transfer to the corresponding spoke in the Serverless Architectures On AWS Scorecard on the second next page of the Self-Assessment.

Your completed Serverless Architectures On AWS Scorecard will give you a clear presentation of which Serverless Architectures On AWS areas need attention.

Serverless Architectures On AWS Scorecard Example

Example of how the finalized Scorecard can look like:

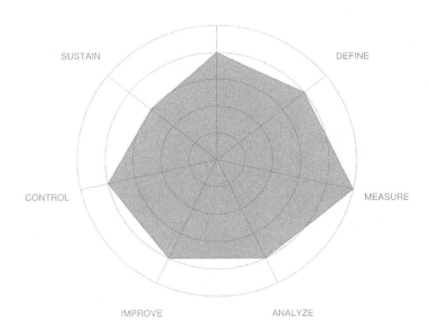

Serverless Architectures On AWS Scorecard

Your Scores:

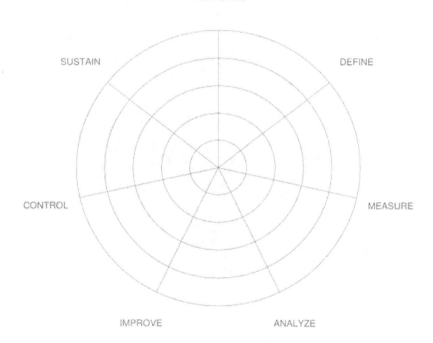

BEGINNING OF THE SELF-ASSESSMENT:

CRITERION #1: RECOGNIZE

INTENT: Be aware of the need for change. Recognize that there is an unfavorable variation, problem or symptom.

In my belief, the answer to this question is clearly defined:

5 Strongly Agree

4 Agree

3 Neutral

2 Disagree

1 Strongly Disagree

1. What information do users need?
<--- Score

2. How do you identify the kinds of information that you will need?
<--- Score

3. Does Serverless Architectures on AWS create potential expectations in other areas that need to be

recognized and considered?

<--- Score

4. What needs to change?

<--- Score

5. Consider your own Serverless Architectures on AWS project, what types of organizational problems do you think might be causing or affecting your problem, based on the work done so far?

<--- Score

6. Do you have/need 24-hour access to key personnel?

<--- Score

7. Is the need for organizational change recognized?

<--- Score

8. What does Serverless Architectures on AWS success mean to the stakeholders?

<--- Score

9. How do you recognize an Serverless Architectures on AWS objection?

<--- Score

10. How can you balance the need for efficiency and exploration with fairness and sensitivity to users?

<--- Score

11. What should be considered when identifying available resources, constraints, and deadlines?

<--- Score

12. Who else hopes to benefit from it?

<--- Score

13. What situation(s) led to this Serverless Architectures on AWS Self Assessment?
<--- Score

14. What is the problem and/or vulnerability?
<--- Score

15. What if you did not need an app server anymore?
<--- Score

16. What are the Serverless Architectures on AWS resources needed?
<--- Score

17. The most common problem in any shared cluster, having run on many of them, is do you have the resources you need when you need them?
<--- Score

18. What Serverless Architectures on AWS problem should be solved?
<--- Score

19. What needs to stay?
<--- Score

20. What technical breakthroughs were needed to make serverless computing possible?
<--- Score

21. How do you identify subcontractor relationships?
<--- Score

22. What needs to be done?
<--- Score

23. Which information does the Serverless Architectures on AWS business case need to include?
<--- Score

24. How are you going to measure success?
<--- Score

25. What problems are you trying to solve?
<--- Score

26. Can management personnel recognize the monetary benefit of Serverless Architectures on AWS?
<--- Score

27. What are the expected benefits of Serverless Architectures on AWS to the stakeholder?
<--- Score

28. What is the recognized need?
<--- Score

29. How are the Serverless Architectures on AWS's objectives aligned to the group's overall stakeholder strategy?
<--- Score

30. Will new equipment/products be required to facilitate Serverless Architectures on AWS delivery, for example is new software needed?
<--- Score

31. What knowledge of distributed systems and

networking does a FaaS user still need to know?
<--- Score

32. Which AWS services is not supported as an AWS lambda event source?
<--- Score

33. How do you assess your Serverless Architectures on AWS workforce capability and capacity needs, including skills, competencies, and staffing levels?
<--- Score

34. How many servers do you need?
<--- Score

35. What are the timeframes required to resolve each of the issues/problems?
<--- Score

36. What is the extent or complexity of the Serverless Architectures on AWS problem?
<--- Score

37. What triggers code execution?
<--- Score

38. Are there any specific expectations or concerns about the Serverless Architectures on AWS team, Serverless Architectures on AWS itself?
<--- Score

39. Why do you need a new paradigm?
<--- Score

40. Why the need?
<--- Score

41. What do you need to start doing?
<--- Score

42. What is your strategy on asynchronous calls and events within your serverless architecture?
<--- Score

43. When a Serverless Architectures on AWS manager recognizes a problem, what options are available?
<--- Score

44. What extra resources will you need?
<--- Score

45. When is new tooling needed where?
<--- Score

46. Do you have a problem with using something that you can not audit?
<--- Score

47. Does serverless need to have IaaS-like based pricing?
<--- Score

48. How do you detect and investigate security events?
<--- Score

49. What problems are you facing and how do you consider Serverless Architectures on AWS will circumvent those obstacles?
<--- Score

50. How do you manage workload and operations

events?
<--- Score

51. What are the things you are going to need?
<--- Score

52. How to build a serverless application with the least amount of code needed?
<--- Score

53. What are the stakeholder objectives to be achieved with Serverless Architectures on AWS?
<--- Score

54. What are your needs in relation to Serverless Architectures on AWS skills, labor, equipment, and markets?
<--- Score

55. What if you need to invoke two, three, or more Lambda functions at the same time?
<--- Score

56. Who are your key stakeholders who need to sign off?
<--- Score

57. As a sponsor, customer or management, how important is it to meet goals, objectives?
<--- Score

58. How much are sponsors, customers, partners, stakeholders involved in Serverless Architectures on AWS? In other words, what are the risks, if Serverless Architectures on AWS does not deliver successfully?
<--- Score

59. What Serverless Architectures on AWS events should you attend?
<--- Score

60. What would happen if Serverless Architectures on AWS weren't done?
<--- Score

61. Are there regulatory / compliance issues?
<--- Score

62. Can you see a single view of issues across all your servers and applications?
<--- Score

Add up total points for this section:
_ _ _ _ _ = Total points for this section

Divided by: _ _ _ _ _ _ (number of statements answered) = _ _ _ _ _ _
Average score for this section

Transfer your score to the Serverless Architectures on AWS Index at the beginning of the Self-Assessment.

CRITERION #2: DEFINE:

INTENT: Formulate the stakeholder problem. Define the problem, needs and objectives.

In my belief, the answer to this question is clearly defined:

5 Strongly Agree

4 Agree

3 Neutral

2 Disagree

1 Strongly Disagree

1. Are required metrics defined, what are they?
<--- Score

2. How do you manage changes in Serverless Architectures on AWS requirements?
<--- Score

3. Is the team formed and are team leaders (Coaches and Management Leads) assigned?

<--- Score

4. What are the rough order estimates on cost savings/
opportunities that Serverless Architectures on AWS
brings?
<--- Score

5. Are accountability and ownership for Serverless
Architectures on AWS clearly defined?
<--- Score

6. How do you think the partners involved in
Serverless Architectures on AWS would have defined
success?
<--- Score

7. Has the direction changed at all during the course
of Serverless Architectures on AWS? If so, when did it
change and why?
<--- Score

8. Is there a Serverless Architectures on AWS
management charter, including stakeholder case,
problem and goal statements, scope, milestones, roles
and responsibilities, communication plan?
<--- Score

9. When is/was the Serverless Architectures on AWS
start date?
<--- Score

10. When is the estimated completion date?
<--- Score

11. How is the team tracking and documenting its
work?

<--- Score

12. Is Serverless Architectures on AWS linked to key stakeholder goals and objectives?
<--- Score

13. Are customers identified and high impact areas defined?
<--- Score

14. What is the worst case scenario?
<--- Score

15. What knowledge or experience is required?
<--- Score

16. Has the Serverless Architectures on AWS work been fairly and/or equitably divided and delegated among team members who are qualified and capable to perform the work? Has everyone contributed?
<--- Score

17. What are the Serverless Architectures on AWS tasks and definitions?
<--- Score

18. What intelligence can you gather?
<--- Score

19. What critical content must be communicated – who, what, when, where, and how?
<--- Score

20. What are the compelling stakeholder reasons for embarking on Serverless Architectures on AWS?
<--- Score

21. What are the tasks and definitions?
<--- Score

22. Has a team charter been developed and communicated?
<--- Score

23. Are improvement team members fully trained on Serverless Architectures on AWS?
<--- Score

24. Has a project plan, Gantt chart, or similar been developed/completed?
<--- Score

25. What information do you gather?
<--- Score

26. Are stakeholder processes mapped?
<--- Score

27. Why would you use Amazon Aurora over, for example, SQL with Amazon RDS?
<--- Score

28. Are team charters developed?
<--- Score

29. How will the Serverless Architectures on AWS team and the group measure complete success of Serverless Architectures on AWS?
<--- Score

30. How was the 'as is' process map developed, reviewed, verified and validated?

<--- Score

31. Is the Serverless Architectures on AWS scope manageable?
<--- Score

32. Is Serverless Architectures on AWS currently on schedule according to the plan?
<--- Score

33. How do you gather the stories?
<--- Score

34. Is any Serverless Architectures on AWS documentation required?
<--- Score

35. Has/have the customer(s) been identified?
<--- Score

36. How do you deliver the required availability?
<--- Score

37. Has anyone else (internal or external to the group) attempted to solve this problem or a similar one before? If so, what knowledge can be leveraged from these previous efforts?
<--- Score

38. Who is gathering information?
<--- Score

39. Will team members perform Serverless Architectures on AWS work when assigned and in a timely fashion?
<--- Score

40. Who are the Serverless Architectures on AWS improvement team members, including Management Leads and Coaches?
<--- Score

41. What are the Serverless Architectures on AWS use cases?
<--- Score

42. Is there a critical path to deliver Serverless Architectures on AWS results?
<--- Score

43. If substitutes have been appointed, have they been briefed on the Serverless Architectures on AWS goals and received regular communications as to the progress to date?
<--- Score

44. Are approval levels defined for contracts and supplements to contracts?
<--- Score

45. What sources do you use to gather information for a Serverless Architectures on AWS study?
<--- Score

46. Is there regularly 100% attendance at the team meetings? If not, have appointed substitutes attended to preserve cross-functionality and full representation?
<--- Score

47. Does the team have regular meetings?
<--- Score

48. When are meeting minutes sent out? Who is on the distribution list?
<--- Score

49. How are consistent Serverless Architectures on AWS definitions important?
<--- Score

50. What are the record-keeping requirements of Serverless Architectures on AWS activities?
<--- Score

51. What are the dynamics of the communication plan?
<--- Score

52. Have all basic functions of Serverless Architectures on AWS been defined?
<--- Score

53. What scope to assess?
<--- Score

54. Has everyone on the team, including the team leaders, been properly trained?
<--- Score

55. Are there different segments of customers?
<--- Score

56. What kind of functionality do you require?
<--- Score

57. Has a high-level 'as is' process map been completed, verified and validated?

<--- Score

58. How do you gather requirements?
<--- Score

59. Has the improvement team collected the 'voice of the customer' (obtained feedback – qualitative and quantitative)?
<--- Score

60. What are your latency requirements?
<--- Score

61. How can the value of Serverless Architectures on AWS be defined?
<--- Score

62. What are the requirements for the DevOps pipeline for Serverless applications?
<--- Score

63. What is the definition of success?
<--- Score

64. Is data collected and displayed to better understand customer(s) critical needs and requirements.
<--- Score

65. What constraints exist that might impact the team?
<--- Score

66. How will variation in the actual durations of each activity be dealt with to ensure that the expected Serverless Architectures on AWS results are met?

<--- Score

67. Has a Serverless Architectures on AWS requirement not been met?
<--- Score

68. How well does the implemented DevOps pipeline fulfil business requirements?
<--- Score

69. How do you keep key subject matter experts in the loop?
<--- Score

70. What key stakeholder process output measure(s) does Serverless Architectures on AWS leverage and how?
<--- Score

71. What baselines are required to be defined and managed?
<--- Score

72. Do architectural changes in test require coordinating disparate templates for prod or can it be done visually and automatically?
<--- Score

73. How did the Serverless Architectures on AWS manager receive input to the development of a Serverless Architectures on AWS improvement plan and the estimated completion dates/times of each activity?
<--- Score

74. Will team members regularly document their

Serverless Architectures on AWS work?
<--- Score

75. How do you manage unclear Serverless Architectures on AWS requirements?
<--- Score

76. Have the customer needs been translated into specific, measurable requirements? How?
<--- Score

77. Is the team adequately staffed with the desired cross-functionality? If not, what additional resources are available to the team?
<--- Score

78. Are customer(s) identified and segmented according to their different needs and requirements?
<--- Score

79. How often are the team meetings?
<--- Score

80. How does the Serverless Architectures on AWS manager ensure against scope creep?
<--- Score

81. Is the improvement team aware of the different versions of a process: what they think it is vs. what it actually is vs. what it should be vs. what it could be?
<--- Score

82. Is full participation by members in regularly held team meetings guaranteed?
<--- Score

83. What would be the goal or target for a Serverless Architectures on AWS's improvement team?
<--- Score

84. What are the Roles and Responsibilities for each team member and its leadership? Where is this documented?
<--- Score

85. Is the current 'as is' process being followed? If not, what are the discrepancies?
<--- Score

86. What are the boundaries of the scope? What is in bounds and what is not? What is the start point? What is the stop point?
<--- Score

87. Are different versions of process maps needed to account for the different types of inputs?
<--- Score

88. What is in scope?
<--- Score

89. Is the work to date meeting requirements?
<--- Score

90. Is a fully trained team formed, supported, and committed to work on the Serverless Architectures on AWS improvements?
<--- Score

91. Is there a completed, verified, and validated high-level 'as is' (not 'should be' or 'could be') stakeholder process map?

<--- Score

92. How do you manage scope?
<--- Score

93. What customer feedback methods were used to solicit their input?
<--- Score

94. What specifically is the problem? Where does it occur? When does it occur? What is its extent?
<--- Score

95. Are audit criteria, scope, frequency and methods defined?
<--- Score

96. Will a Serverless Architectures on AWS production readiness review be required?
<--- Score

97. Are there any constraints known that bear on the ability to perform Serverless Architectures on AWS work? How is the team addressing them?
<--- Score

98. What types of technical use cases are serverless technologies being used for?
<--- Score

99. Is the team equipped with available and reliable resources?
<--- Score

100. Is there a completed SIPOC representation, describing the Suppliers, Inputs, Process, Outputs, and

Customers?

<--- Score

101. What is out-of-scope initially?

<--- Score

102. Do the problem and goal statements meet the SMART criteria (specific, measurable, attainable, relevant, and time-bound)?

<--- Score

103. Is the team sponsored by a champion or stakeholder leader?

<--- Score

104. What sort of initial information to gather?

<--- Score

Add up total points for this section:
_____ = Total points for this section

Divided by: _____ (number of statements answered) = _____
Average score for this section

Transfer your score to the Serverless Architectures on AWS Index at the beginning of the Self-Assessment.

CRITERION #3: MEASURE:

INTENT: Gather the correct data.
Measure the current performance and
evolution of the situation.

In my belief, the answer to this
question is clearly defined:

5 Strongly Agree

4 Agree

3 Neutral

2 Disagree

1 Strongly Disagree

**1. How do you prioritize inclusion as you build
your technical teams?**
<--- Score

2. What are the agreed upon definitions of the high
impact areas, defect(s), unit(s), and opportunities that
will figure into the process capability metrics?
<--- Score

3. Does your organization systematically track and analyze outcomes related for accountability and quality improvement?
<--- Score

4. What has the team done to assure the stability and accuracy of the measurement process?
<--- Score

5. Do the benefits outweigh the costs?
<--- Score

6. How do you use pricing models to reduce cost?
<--- Score

7. Was a data collection plan established?
<--- Score

8. What does verifying compliance entail?
<--- Score

9. How do you identify and analyze stakeholders and their interests?
<--- Score

10. Is service priority useful in networks?
<--- Score

11. Are there measurements based on task performance?
<--- Score

12. Are the measurements objective?
<--- Score

13. Where should developers focus time and

money now?
<--- Score

14. Is data collection planned and executed?
<--- Score

15. Who participated in the data collection for measurements?
<--- Score

16. Are process variation components displayed/ communicated using suitable charts, graphs, plots?
<--- Score

17. How are you verifying it?
<--- Score

18. Is data collected on key measures that were identified?
<--- Score

19. Are actual costs in line with budgeted costs?
<--- Score

20. How are you evolving your serverless application while minimizing the impact of change?
<--- Score

21. What measurements are being captured?
<--- Score

22. What are the associated database technology license costs?
<--- Score

23. Where is the cost?
<--- Score

24. What does a Test Case verify?
<--- Score

25. Do you aggressively reward and promote the people who have the biggest impact on creating excellent Serverless Architectures on AWS services/ products?
<--- Score

26. What are hidden Serverless Architectures on AWS quality costs?
<--- Score

27. How are measurements made?
<--- Score

28. What are the costs of reform?
<--- Score

29. What is the root cause(s) of the problem?
<--- Score

30. How do you evaluate cost when you select services?
<--- Score

31. What causes production sprawl?
<--- Score

32. Is key measure data collection planned and executed, process variation displayed and communicated and performance baselined?
<--- Score

33. What are your customers expectations and measures?
<--- Score

34. What tests verify requirements?
<--- Score

35. How can you reduce costs?
<--- Score

36. What is the real impact of the system being unavailable?
<--- Score

37. What are the operational costs after Serverless Architectures on AWS deployment?
<--- Score

38. How do you verify and develop ideas and innovations?
<--- Score

39. What is the cost of rework?
<--- Score

40. How do you focus on what is right -not who is right?
<--- Score

41. Which stakeholder characteristics are analyzed?
<--- Score

42. What charts has the team used to display the components of variation in the process?
<--- Score

43. Do you have any cost Serverless Architectures on AWS limitation requirements?
<--- Score

44. How do you stay flexible and focused to recognize larger Serverless Architectures on AWS results?
<--- Score

45. What could cause you to change course?
<--- Score

46. What priorities should the OIT Cloud Team focus on to move everyone forward?
<--- Score

47. What would be a real cause for concern?
<--- Score

48. What does losing customers cost your organization?
<--- Score

49. Is the cost worth the Serverless Architectures on AWS effort ?
<--- Score

50. What particular quality tools did the team find helpful in establishing measurements?
<--- Score

51. How sensitive must the Serverless Architectures on AWS strategy be to cost?
<--- Score

52. What is the cause of any Serverless Architectures

on AWS gaps?
<--- Score

53. Is there an opportunity to verify requirements?
<--- Score

54. Who should receive measurement reports?
<--- Score

55. What disadvantage does this cause for the user?
<--- Score

56. Are you able to realize any cost savings?
<--- Score

57. Have changes been properly/adequately analyzed
for effect?
<--- Score

58. How large is the gap between current
performance and the customer-specified (goal)
performance?
<--- Score

59. What is your Serverless Architectures on AWS
quality cost segregation study?
<--- Score

60. Is there a Performance Baseline?
<--- Score

61. What are the types and number of measures to
use?
<--- Score

62. Are there competing Serverless Architectures on

AWS priorities?

<--- Score

63. How fair is queue prioritization?

<--- Score

64. Is the scope of Serverless Architectures on AWS cost analysis cost-effective?

<--- Score

65. Are high impact defects defined and identified in the stakeholder process?

<--- Score

66. Is a follow-up focused external Serverless Architectures on AWS review required?

<--- Score

67. Do you want to optimize for speed to market or for cost?

<--- Score

68. Do you want to prioritize for speed to market or for cost?

<--- Score

69. What are the Serverless Architectures on AWS investment costs?

<--- Score

70. How is the value delivered by Serverless Architectures on AWS being measured?

<--- Score

71. What is the total fixed cost?

<--- Score

72. How are you analyzing serverless application logs?
<--- Score

73. What data was collected (past, present, future/ongoing)?
<--- Score

74. What harm might be caused?
<--- Score

75. How does the cloud impact and interface with the goals of IT Optimization?
<--- Score

76. What users will be impacted?
<--- Score

77. How does cost-to-serve analysis help?
<--- Score

78. How do you determine what your priorities are?
<--- Score

79. Are indirect costs charged to the Serverless Architectures on AWS program?
<--- Score

80. What key measures identified indicate the performance of the stakeholder process?
<--- Score

81. Is there any ability to prioritize messages or setup a predetermined order?

<--- Score

82. How to model and analyze gossiping protocols?
<--- Score

83. Are key measures identified and agreed upon?
<--- Score

84. What is the right balance of time and resources between investigation, analysis, and discussion and dissemination?
<--- Score

85. Is Process Variation Displayed/Communicated?
<--- Score

86. Are Serverless Architectures on AWS vulnerabilities categorized and prioritized?
<--- Score

87. Have you made assumptions about the shape of the future, particularly its impact on your customers and competitors?
<--- Score

88. What does your operating model cost?
<--- Score

89. What is the total cost related to deploying Serverless Architectures on AWS, including any consulting or professional services?
<--- Score

90. Do you verify that corrective actions were taken?
<--- Score

91. How do you do risk analysis of rare, cascading, catastrophic events?
<--- Score

92. Are there any easy-to-implement alternatives to Serverless Architectures on AWS? Sometimes other solutions are available that do not require the cost implications of a full-blown project?
<--- Score

93. Have you found any 'ground fruit' or 'low-hanging fruit' for immediate remedies to the gap in performance?
<--- Score

94. What are the key input variables? What are the key process variables? What are the key output variables?
<--- Score

95. What kind of analytics data will be gathered?
<--- Score

96. What do you measure and why?
<--- Score

97. Can you measure the return on analysis?
<--- Score

98. How will you measure your Serverless Architectures on AWS effectiveness?
<--- Score

99. How much aggressiveness can cause instability?
<--- Score

100. What are the costs involved in switching to serverless?
<--- Score

101. What is your cost benefit analysis?
<--- Score

102. Is long term and short term variability accounted for?
<--- Score

103. Has a cost center been established?
<--- Score

104. How do you meet cost targets when you select resource type and size?
<--- Score

105. How can you measure Serverless Architectures on AWS in a systematic way?
<--- Score

106. Where can you go to verify the info?
<--- Score

107. Does Serverless Architectures on AWS analysis show the relationships among important Serverless Architectures on AWS factors?
<--- Score

108. Is a solid data collection plan established that includes measurement systems analysis?
<--- Score

109. Was a business case (cost/benefit) developed?

<--- Score

Add up total points for this section:
_____ = Total points for this section

Divided by: _____ (number of
statements answered) = _____
Average score for this section

Transfer your score to the Serverless
Architectures on AWS Index at the
beginning of the Self-Assessment.

CRITERION #4: ANALYZE:

INTENT: Analyze causes, assumptions and hypotheses.

In my belief, the answer to this question is clearly defined:

5 Strongly Agree

4 Agree

3 Neutral

2 Disagree

1 Strongly Disagree

1. What is your data model and how are you going to query the data?
<--- Score

2. Have you defined which data is gathered how?
<--- Score

3. How do you drive public cloud adoption for a massive organization charged with providing excellent service to clients?

<--- Score

4. What internal processes need improvement?
<--- Score

5. What Serverless Architectures on AWS data will be collected?
<--- Score

6. Were any designed experiments used to generate additional insight into the data analysis?
<--- Score

7. Should you invest in industry-recognized qualifications?
<--- Score

8. When should a process be art not science?
<--- Score

9. How do you protect your data at rest?
<--- Score

10. What controls do you have in place to protect data?
<--- Score

11. Which Serverless Architectures on AWS data should be retained?
<--- Score

12. Have any additional benefits been identified that will result from closing all or most of the gaps?
<--- Score

13. Who gets your output?

<--- Score

14. Were Pareto charts (or similar) used to portray the 'heavy hitters' (or key sources of variation)?
<--- Score

15. What quality tools were used to get through the analyze phase?
<--- Score

16. Were there any improvement opportunities identified from the process analysis?
<--- Score

17. Are all team members qualified for all tasks?
<--- Score

18. What are evaluation criteria for the output?
<--- Score

19. Who is involved in the management review process?
<--- Score

20. What resources go in to get the desired output?
<--- Score

21. Do you, as a leader, bounce back quickly from setbacks?
<--- Score

22. How are you protecting sensitive data within your serverless application?
<--- Score

23. Where is Serverless Architectures on AWS data

gathered?
<--- Score

24. What were the crucial 'moments of truth' on the process map?
<--- Score

25. How do you classify your data?
<--- Score

26. Where is all this data going to go?
<--- Score

27. How do you protect your data in transit?
<--- Score

28. If you were to map your different workload types; the batch, the daemon, your organizationful and your organizationless, to compute mediums on AWS, what does that mapping look like?
<--- Score

29. How difficult is it to qualify what Serverless Architectures on AWS ROI is?
<--- Score

30. How quickly will that solution help you troubleshoot issues in your particular system?
<--- Score

31. What data do you need to collect?
<--- Score

32. Are your outputs consistent?
<--- Score

33. Where is the data going?
<--- Score

34. How much data will you need to store and for how long?
<--- Score

35. What are the processes for audit reporting and management?
<--- Score

36. What does cloud first really mean for your processes, customers, and the future of your business?
<--- Score

37. How do you select your database solution?
<--- Score

38. What is the cost of poor quality as supported by the team's analysis?
<--- Score

39. What Serverless Architectures on AWS data do you gather or use now?
<--- Score

40. Has an output goal been set?
<--- Score

41. Do staff qualifications match your project?
<--- Score

42. Is there an established change management process?
<--- Score

43. What are your key performance measures or indicators and in-process measures for the control and improvement of your Serverless Architectures on AWS processes?
<--- Score

44. Is the final output clearly identified?
<--- Score

45. Are gaps between current performance and the goal performance identified?
<--- Score

46. What tools were used to generate the list of possible causes?
<--- Score

47. How to transfer data between tasks?
<--- Score

48. What types of data do your Serverless Architectures on AWS indicators require?
<--- Score

49. Who will facilitate the team and process?
<--- Score

50. How do you deal with your data?
<--- Score

51. What are the requirements in terms of durability of data?
<--- Score

52. Which functions will handle sensitive data and

where is it stored?
<--- Score

53. Was a detailed process map created to amplify critical steps of the 'as is' stakeholder process?
<--- Score

54. Have the problem and goal statements been updated to reflect the additional knowledge gained from the analyze phase?
<--- Score

55. What does the data say about the performance of the stakeholder process?
<--- Score

56. How are you initializing database connections?
<--- Score

57. How can risk management be tied procedurally to process elements?
<--- Score

58. What output to create?
<--- Score

59. What do you need to qualify?
<--- Score

60. Can you add value to the current Serverless Architectures on AWS decision-making process (largely qualitative) by incorporating uncertainty modeling (more quantitative)?
<--- Score

61. What kind of crime could a potential new hire

have committed that would not only not disqualify him/her from being hired by your organization, but would actually indicate that he/she might be a particularly good fit?
<--- Score

62. Do your leaders quickly bounce back from setbacks?
<--- Score

63. Did any value-added analysis or 'lean thinking' take place to identify some of the gaps shown on the 'as is' process map?
<--- Score

64. Is data and process analysis, root cause analysis and quantifying the gap/opportunity in place?
<--- Score

65. How are outputs preserved and protected?
<--- Score

66. What information qualified as important?
<--- Score

67. Personnel: when additional engineers are added to a team, how quickly can they rampup, coordinating changes, and collaborate?
<--- Score

68. Where does the data live in all this?
<--- Score

69. How was the detailed process map generated, verified, and validated?
<--- Score

70. Did any additional data need to be collected?
<--- Score

71. Is the gap/opportunity displayed and communicated in financial terms?
<--- Score

72. Where can you get qualified talent today?
<--- Score

73. What tools were used to narrow the list of possible causes?
<--- Score

74. What are your outputs?
<--- Score

75. Do several people in different organizational units assist with the Serverless Architectures on AWS process?
<--- Score

76. What conclusions were drawn from the team's data collection and analysis? How did the team reach these conclusions?
<--- Score

77. What were the financial benefits resulting from any 'ground fruit or low-hanging fruit' (quick fixes)?
<--- Score

78. How is the data gathered?
<--- Score

79. How do you back up data?

<--- Score

80. Do you have the authority to produce the output?
<--- Score

81. What is the complexity of the output produced?
<--- Score

82. What is an event-driven architecture?
<--- Score

83. Are any processes running that you do not expect?
<--- Score

84. What did the team gain from developing a sub-process map?
<--- Score

85. What are the personnel training and qualifications required?
<--- Score

86. Is it technically feasible to automate this process?
<--- Score

87. What is an effective development process (workflow) for applications of cloud-functions?
<--- Score

88. Is the performance gap determined?
<--- Score

89. What happens when advanced services, access controls, and databases are added?

<--- Score

90. What is the Value Stream Mapping?
<--- Score

91. Was a cause-and-effect diagram used to explore the different types of causes (or sources of variation)?
<--- Score

92. Identify an operational issue in your organization, for example, could a particular task be done more quickly or more efficiently by Serverless Architectures on AWS?
<--- Score

93. Who is involved with workflow mapping?
<--- Score

94. What are the revised rough estimates of the financial savings/opportunity for Serverless Architectures on AWS improvements?
<--- Score

95. How do you promote understanding that opportunity for improvement is not criticism of the status quo, or the people who created the status quo?
<--- Score

96. Traceability, do teams need to be able to answer questions like which data was this model trained on?
<--- Score

97. Is the Serverless Architectures on AWS process severely broken such that a re-design is necessary?
<--- Score

Add up total points for this section:
_ _ _ _ _ = Total points for this section

Divided by: _ _ _ _ _ _ (number of
statements answered) = _ _ _ _ _ _
Average score for this section

Transfer your score to the Serverless
Architectures on AWS Index at the
beginning of the Self-Assessment.

CRITERION #5: IMPROVE:

INTENT: Develop a practical solution. Innovate, establish and test the solution and to measure the results.

In my belief, the answer to this question is clearly defined:

5 Strongly Agree

4 Agree

3 Neutral

2 Disagree

1 Strongly Disagree

1. What does the 'should be' process map/design look like?
<--- Score

2. Can you identify any significant risks or exposures to Serverless Architectures on AWS third- parties (vendors, service providers, alliance partners etc) that concern you?
<--- Score

3. Will the controls trigger any other risks?
<--- Score

4. Are there any constraints (technical, political, cultural, or otherwise) that would inhibit certain solutions?
<--- Score

5. Is pilot data collected and analyzed?
<--- Score

6. How do you measure risk?
<--- Score

7. What tools were most useful during the improve phase?
<--- Score

8. How do you configure your networking solution?
<--- Score

9. What resources are required for the improvement efforts?
<--- Score

10. What communications are necessary to support the implementation of the solution?
<--- Score

11. Do you believe your organizations security posture has been improved by serverless?
<--- Score

12. Is a solution implementation plan established,

including schedule/work breakdown structure, resources, risk management plan, cost/budget, and control plan?
<--- Score

13. When a product as Lambda poses powerful possibilities in the public sphere, at what point is developers ease-of-use a liability for the people?
<--- Score

14. Are the key business and technology risks being managed?
<--- Score

15. How do you understand the health of your operations?
<--- Score

16. Are you still operating with yesterdays model where there is infrastructure teams who touch the infrastructure and the application teams who develop the code?
<--- Score

17. Explorations of the frontiers of Serverless Architectures on AWS will help you build influence, improve Serverless Architectures on AWS, optimize decision making, and sustain change, what is your approach?
<--- Score

18. Are the most efficient solutions problem-specific?
<--- Score

19. What were the underlying assumptions on the cost-benefit analysis?

<--- Score

20. What are the implications of the one critical Serverless Architectures on AWS decision 10 minutes, 10 months, and 10 years from now?
<--- Score

21. Why do you need new solutions?
<--- Score

22. Who are the Serverless Architectures on AWS decision-makers?
<--- Score

23. Are you assessing Serverless Architectures on AWS and risk?
<--- Score

24. Describe the design of the pilot and what tests were conducted, if any?
<--- Score

25. What is your strategy for deciding the most optimal lambda memory allocation?
<--- Score

26. How do you decide how much to remunerate an employee?
<--- Score

27. Which Serverless Architectures on AWS solution is appropriate?
<--- Score

28. What error proofing will be done to address some of the discrepancies observed in the 'as is' process?

<--- Score

29. What went well, what should change, what can improve?
<--- Score

30. Where do the Serverless Architectures on AWS decisions reside?
<--- Score

31. How do you understand the health of your workload?
<--- Score

32. How will the team or the process owner(s) monitor the implementation plan to see that it is working as intended?
<--- Score

33. What tools were used to evaluate the potential solutions?
<--- Score

34. How to decompose apps into functions so that they user resources optimally?
<--- Score

35. Is the Serverless Architectures on AWS risk managed?
<--- Score

36. Which techniques are helpful to better understand the mental model behind FaaS?
<--- Score

37. Was a pilot designed for the proposed solution(s)?

<--- Score

38. How do you select your compute solution?
<--- Score

39. Does your organization have the resourcing internally to both keep current applications running smoothly as well as improving them in response to changing needs?
<--- Score

40. Do vendor agreements bring new compliance risk ?
<--- Score

41. How does serverless improve security?
<--- Score

42. Who manages supplier risk management in your organization?
<--- Score

43. Have you achieved Serverless Architectures on AWS improvements?
<--- Score

44. Serverless Architectures on AWS risk decisions: whose call Is It?
<--- Score

45. How are policy decisions made and where?
<--- Score

46. Who are the key stakeholders for the Serverless Architectures on AWS evaluation?
<--- Score

47. What are the expected Serverless Architectures on AWS results?
<--- Score

48. To what extent does management recognize Serverless Architectures on AWS as a tool to increase the results?
<--- Score

49. How do you mitigate deployment risks?
<--- Score

50. What actually has to improve and by how much?
<--- Score

51. What alternative responses are available to manage risk?
<--- Score

52. Should deployment be optimized?
<--- Score

53. If serverless is so secure, why do you need new solutions?
<--- Score

54. Is there a high likelihood that any recommendations will achieve their intended results?
<--- Score

55. Are possible solutions generated and tested?
<--- Score

56. Is the optimal solution selected based on testing and analysis?

<--- Score

57. How have you optimized the performance of your serverless application?
<--- Score

58. Is a contingency plan established?
<--- Score

59. Is the Serverless Architectures on AWS solution sustainable?
<--- Score

60. How will the group know that the solution worked?
<--- Score

61. What lessons, if any, from a pilot were incorporated into the design of the full-scale solution?
<--- Score

62. How often do you map your network?
<--- Score

63. How do you decide what components of your serverless application should be deployed?
<--- Score

64. Who will be using the results of the measurement activities?
<--- Score

65. What strategies for Serverless Architectures on AWS improvement are successful?
<--- Score

66. Are the risks fully understood, reasonable and manageable?
<--- Score

67. Were any criteria developed to assist the team in testing and evaluating potential solutions?
<--- Score

68. As the rate of change accelerates, and the complexity of projects increases, how can Developers innovate and build faster?
<--- Score

69. How is continuous improvement applied to risk management?
<--- Score

70. What is the team's contingency plan for potential problems occurring in implementation?
<--- Score

71. How do multiple developers/teams collaborate on serverless applications?
<--- Score

72. How are you optimizing your code to run in the least amount of time possible?
<--- Score

73. In the past few months, what is the smallest change you have made that has had the biggest positive result? What was it about that small change that produced the large return?
<--- Score

74. How has development changed?

<--- Score

75. What to do with the results or outcomes of measurements?
<--- Score

76. What functions are still being developed?
<--- Score

77. How do you use tradeoffs to improve performance?
<--- Score

78. What criteria will you use to assess your Serverless Architectures on AWS risks?
<--- Score

79. Do you understand how operating model changes are key to cloud adoption?
<--- Score

80. How will you know that you have improved?
<--- Score

81. What attendant changes will need to be made to ensure that the solution is successful?
<--- Score

82. Are the best solutions selected?
<--- Score

83. How do you improve productivity?
<--- Score

84. When you map the key players in your own work and the types/domains of relationships with them,

which relationships do you find easy and which challenging, and why?
<--- Score

85. Who are the Serverless Architectures on AWS decision makers?
<--- Score

86. Who makes the Serverless Architectures on AWS decisions in your organization?
<--- Score

87. If there are multiple good options, how to evaluate the pros and cons for a particular workload?
<--- Score

88. How will you know that a change is an improvement?
<--- Score

89. How risky is your organization?
<--- Score

90. Is the implementation plan designed?
<--- Score

91. How do you reduce defects, ease remediation, and improve flow into production?
<--- Score

92. How do you choose the most optimum capacity units (memory, shards, reads/writes per second) within your serverless application?
<--- Score

93. How do you select your storage solution?
<--- Score

94. How are you optimizing your lambda code for performance?
<--- Score

95. Risk events: what are the things that could go wrong?
<--- Score

96. How are you optimizing your lambda functions to reduce overall execution time?
<--- Score

97. What is the implementation plan?
<--- Score

98. Is there a small-scale pilot for proposed improvement(s)? What conclusions were drawn from the outcomes of a pilot?
<--- Score

99. Do you see patterns for building serverless solutions?
<--- Score

100. How will you know when its improved?
<--- Score

101. Is cyber risk really any different in the cloud?
<--- Score

102. If you could go back in time five years, what decision would you make differently? What is your best guess as to what decision you're making today

you might regret five years from now?
<--- Score

103. Who will be responsible for making the decisions to include or exclude requested changes once Serverless Architectures on AWS is underway?
<--- Score

104. Is there a cost/benefit analysis of optimal solution(s)?
<--- Score

105. How do you manage and improve your Serverless Architectures on AWS work systems to deliver customer value and achieve organizational success and sustainability?
<--- Score

106. Are new and improved process ('should be') maps developed?
<--- Score

107. How did the team generate the list of possible solutions?
<--- Score

108. Why amazon aurora for modern application development?
<--- Score

109. What tools were used to tap into the creativity and encourage 'outside the box' thinking?
<--- Score

110. Which is the optimal approach, and why?
<--- Score

111. What is Serverless Architectures on AWS's impact on utilizing the best solution(s)?

<--- Score

112. How does the solution remove the key sources of issues discovered in the analyze phase?

<--- Score

113. What are the affordable Serverless Architectures on AWS risks?

<--- Score

114. How do you design your workload so that you can understand its state?

<--- Score

115. What operational concerns still matter to the developer?

<--- Score

116. What practices helps your organization to develop its capacity to recognize patterns?

<--- Score

117. Who should make the Serverless Architectures on AWS decisions?

<--- Score

118. Can large disk built-in caches really improve system performance?

<--- Score

119. How do you evaluate new services?

<--- Score

120. Are improved process ('should be') maps modified based on pilot data and analysis?
<--- Score

121. How do you measure progress and evaluate training effectiveness?
<--- Score

122. Is risk periodically assessed?
<--- Score

123. At what point will vulnerability assessments be performed once Serverless Architectures on AWS is put into production (e.g., ongoing Risk Management after implementation)?
<--- Score

Add up total points for this section:
_____ = Total points for this section

Divided by: _____ (number of statements answered) = _____
Average score for this section

Transfer your score to the Serverless Architectures on AWS Index at the beginning of the Self-Assessment.

CRITERION #6: CONTROL:

INTENT: Implement the practical solution. Maintain the performance and correct possible complications.

In my belief, the answer to this question is clearly defined:

5 Strongly Agree

4 Agree

3 Neutral

2 Disagree

1 Strongly Disagree

1. How will you measure your QA plan's effectiveness?
<--- Score

2. Can your organization adjust to the rapid changes in technology and applications?
<--- Score

3. Have you recently taken part in the planning phase of a new application ?

<--- Score

4. What other systems, operations, processes, and infrastructures (hiring practices, staffing, training, incentives/rewards, metrics/dashboards/scorecards, etc.) need updates, additions, changes, or deletions in order to facilitate knowledge transfer and improvements?
<--- Score

5. How do you control human access?
<--- Score

6. Is there documentation that will support the successful operation of the improvement?
<--- Score

7. Is new knowledge gained imbedded in the response plan?
<--- Score

8. Has the improved process and its steps been standardized?
<--- Score

9. How do you plan for disaster recovery?
<--- Score

10. Are you measuring, monitoring and predicting Serverless Architectures on AWS activities to optimize operations and profitability, and enhancing outcomes?
<--- Score

11. What is the control/monitoring plan?
<--- Score

12. Is fair resource sharing responsible for spreading long delays?
<--- Score

13. When should you decide to scale out your servers?
<--- Score

14. How does the Serverless architecture affect DevOps practices as CI, CD and Monitoring of the application?
<--- Score

15. Do the viable solutions scale to future needs?
<--- Score

16. Is there a standardized process?
<--- Score

17. Have a plan, engineers are ready, now what?
<--- Score

18. Is the Internet traffic bursty in short time scales?
<--- Score

19. Where does security play in all this, and what should you be considering and planning in terms of how security is going to exist in a NoOps world?
<--- Score

20. How do you spread information?
<--- Score

21. How are you monitoring and responding to

anomalies in your serverless application?
<--- Score

22. What are you protecting against?
<--- Score

23. Rel 4: how do you monitor your resources?
<--- Score

24. How do you control programmatic access?
<--- Score

25. What resources will you monitor?
<--- Score

26. What can you control?
<--- Score

27. Is there a transfer of ownership and knowledge to process owner and process team tasked with the responsibilities.
<--- Score

28. What are the known security controls?
<--- Score

29. How will the day-to-day responsibilities for monitoring and continual improvement be transferred from the improvement team to the process owner?
<--- Score

30. Is knowledge gained on process shared and institutionalized?
<--- Score

31. When should you decide to scale up your servers?
<--- Score

32. What should you measure to verify efficiency gains?
<--- Score

33. How is change control managed?
<--- Score

34. Is a response plan established and deployed?
<--- Score

35. How do you monitor your resources to ensure they are performing as expected?
<--- Score

36. Are documented procedures clear and easy to follow for the operators?
<--- Score

37. Does job training on the documented procedures need to be part of the process team's education and training?
<--- Score

38. How is Serverless Architectures on AWS project cost planned, managed, monitored?
<--- Score

39. How do controls support value?
<--- Score

40. What quality tools were useful in the control phase?

<--- Score

41. How do senior leaders actions reflect a commitment to the organizations Serverless Architectures on AWS values?
<--- Score

42. What are the critical parameters to watch?
<--- Score

43. Does a troubleshooting guide exist or is it needed?
<--- Score

44. Will any special training be provided for results interpretation?
<--- Score

45. Does the Serverless Architectures on AWS performance meet the customer's requirements?
<--- Score

46. What are usage plans and api keys?
<--- Score

47. How do you monitor dependency vulnerabilities within your serverless application?
<--- Score

48. Will your goals reflect your program budget?
<--- Score

49. What are your results for key measures or indicators of the accomplishment of your Serverless Architectures on AWS strategy and action plans, including building and strengthening core competencies?

<--- Score

50. What should the next improvement project be that is related to Serverless Architectures on AWS?
<--- Score

51. What key inputs and outputs are being measured on an ongoing basis?
<--- Score

52. How might the group capture best practices and lessons learned so as to leverage improvements?
<--- Score

53. How do you defend against emerging security threats?
<--- Score

54. What are the performance and scale of the Serverless Architectures on AWS tools?
<--- Score

55. How do you provide all internal teams with access to machine learning?
<--- Score

56. How do you scale effectively?
<--- Score

57. What if you do not have control over the client?
<--- Score

58. How often will you monitor such resources?
<--- Score

59. Are suggested corrective/restorative actions

indicated on the response plan for known causes to problems that might surface?

<--- Score

60. What are your standards for validation of measurement-based networking research?

<--- Score

61. What do you stand for--and what are you against?

<--- Score

62. Who is the Serverless Architectures on AWS process owner?

<--- Score

63. How do you automatically scale?

<--- Score

64. Are pertinent alerts monitored, analyzed and distributed to appropriate personnel?

<--- Score

65. Is there a recommended audit plan for routine surveillance inspections of Serverless Architectures on AWS's gains?

<--- Score

66. What do your reports reflect?

<--- Score

67. What is the standard for acceptable Serverless Architectures on AWS performance?

<--- Score

68. Swarm auto-scale: what does it take?

<--- Score

69. How does your operating model change and scale in the cloud?
<--- Score

70. What do you monitor?
<--- Score

71. Are operating procedures consistent?
<--- Score

72. Are controls in place and consistently applied?
<--- Score

73. Is there a control plan in place for sustaining improvements (short and long-term)?
<--- Score

74. Does the response plan contain a definite closed loop continual improvement scheme (e.g., plan-do-check-act)?
<--- Score

75. Are new process steps, standards, and documentation ingrained into normal operations?
<--- Score

76. Why did people claim Capacity Planning is not required for serverless?
<--- Score

77. How many planet-wide leaders should there be?
<--- Score

78. How do your controls stack up?

<--- Score

79. How do you select, collect, align, and integrate Serverless Architectures on AWS data and information for tracking daily operations and overall organizational performance, including progress relative to strategic objectives and action plans?
<--- Score

80. How will report readings be checked to effectively monitor performance?
<--- Score

81. What is the recommended frequency of auditing?
<--- Score

82. You may have created your quality measures at a time when you lacked resources, technology wasn't up to the required standard, or low service levels were the industry norm. Have those circumstances changed?
<--- Score

83. Who sets the Serverless Architectures on AWS standards?
<--- Score

84. What do you measure to verify effectiveness gains?
<--- Score

85. Does Serverless Architectures on AWS appropriately measure and monitor risk?
<--- Score

86. How will the process owner and team be able to

hold the gains?
<--- Score

87. Will existing staff require re-training, for example, to learn new business processes?
<--- Score

88. How do you control access to servers?
<--- Score

89. Is a response plan in place for when the input, process, or output measures indicate an 'out-of-control' condition?
<--- Score

90. How will the process owner verify improvement in present and future sigma levels, process capabilities?
<--- Score

91. How does the software get deployed and what controls determine what code is executing ?
<--- Score

92. Do you monitor the effectiveness of your Serverless Architectures on AWS activities?
<--- Score

93. How will new or emerging customer needs/ requirements be checked/communicated to orient the process toward meeting the new specifications and continually reducing variation?
<--- Score

94. How widespread is its use?
<--- Score

95. How will input, process, and output variables be checked to detect for sub-optimal conditions?
<--- Score

96. What does it take to use serverless functions in Production, with safety, and at scale?
<--- Score

97. How to scale?
<--- Score

98. Have new or revised work instructions resulted?
<--- Score

99. Is the Serverless Architectures on AWS test/ monitoring cost justified?
<--- Score

100. How many vpcs do you plan to use?
<--- Score

101. Who will perform the monitoring tasks?
<--- Score

102. Do you plan to use or continue to use a FaaS service in the future?
<--- Score

103. Is reporting being used or needed?
<--- Score

104. What are the top two pain points for monitoring?
<--- Score

105. Are there documented procedures?

<--- Score

106. Is capacity planning required for serverless?
<--- Score

107. Do you need a new term to replace Capacity Planning ?
<--- Score

108. Implementation Planning: is a pilot needed to test the changes before a full roll out occurs?
<--- Score

109. How do you plan for data transfer charges?
<--- Score

110. How do you monitor usage and cost?
<--- Score

111. Is there a documented and implemented monitoring plan?
<--- Score

112. What other areas of the group might benefit from the Serverless Architectures on AWS team's improvements, knowledge, and learning?
<--- Score

113. Can you adapt and adjust to changing Serverless Architectures on AWS situations?
<--- Score

114. How can you control access from your servers?
<--- Score

115. What monitoring tools will you use?
<--- Score

Add up total points for this section:
_____ = Total points for this section

Divided by: _____ (number of
statements answered) = _____
Average score for this section

Transfer your score to the Serverless
Architectures on AWS Index at the
beginning of the Self-Assessment.

CRITERION #7: SUSTAIN:

INTENT: Retain the benefits.

In my belief, the answer to this question is clearly defined:

5 Strongly Agree

4 Agree

3 Neutral

2 Disagree

1 Strongly Disagree

1. How many servers should you budget for?
<--- Score

2. How would you design transactional fan-out?
<--- Score

3. Which do you consider significant challenges for using FaaS services?
<--- Score

4. Who is responsible for Serverless Architectures on

AWS?
<--- Score

5. How large are the already stated functions in your applications, typically?
<--- Score

6. Are policies up-to-date?
<--- Score

7. When bad code goes bad how do you stop the bleeding?
<--- Score

8. How do you go about securing Serverless Architectures on AWS?
<--- Score

9. Which types of applications is FaaS-based computing used for in todays industrial practice?
<--- Score

10. Do you have the right capabilities and capacities?
<--- Score

11. Are you satisfied with your current role? If not, what is missing from it?
<--- Score

12. Will you be able to handle an unexpected increase in traffic/use of your services?
<--- Score

13. Is your strategy driving your strategy? Or is the way in which you allocate resources driving your strategy?

<--- Score

14. What is your testing strategy for serverless applications?
<--- Score

15. Can multipath mitigate power law delays?
<--- Score

16. How to deal with performance variability of infrastructure?
<--- Score

17. Why not put your workers in the cloud to begin with?
<--- Score

18. Who is responsible for securing the application layer?
<--- Score

19. What are microservices?
<--- Score

20. What is your role in your team?
<--- Score

21. What is an automatic scaling group?
<--- Score

22. What are some common things you are looking for in all runtimes?
<--- Score

23. Security in serverless, what gets better, what gets worse?

<--- Score

24. How do you typically test FaaS functions?
<--- Score

25. When should you bother with diagrams?
<--- Score

26. How do you turn meaningful metrics into visual dashboards?
<--- Score

27. Did you choose to deploy to the cloud ?
<--- Score

28. Should you use this at all or avoid it all together?
<--- Score

29. What are major disadvantages that you currently see?
<--- Score

30. Using burstable instances in the public cloud: why, when and how?
<--- Score

31. Political -is anyone trying to undermine this project?
<--- Score

32. Is serverless always appropriate?
<--- Score

33. Have benefits been optimized with all key stakeholders?

<--- Score

34. How would you go about creating and deploying a function entirely from the command line?
<--- Score

35. What size server is right for your performance?
<--- Score

36. Aws lambda still towers over the competition, and for how much longer?
<--- Score

37. How do you select the best performing architecture?
<--- Score

38. What can one function do to another in the same app?
<--- Score

39. How do you manage service limits?
<--- Score

40. Do you try to get something basic in the beginning?
<--- Score

41. How does this change in a microservice architecture?
<--- Score

42. When to stop testing and start using software?
<--- Score

43. How does memory allocation affect function execution time?

<--- Score

44. What is the future of this going forward?

<--- Score

45. How do you get small teams able to fully manage/run, going at the core principles of DevOps?

<--- Score

46. Security is visible? Who is accessing the resources?

<--- Score

47. What are the limits of concurrency that you can expect?

<--- Score

48. How do you choose what goes into a function?

<--- Score

49. How do you correlate serverless across your whole architecture?

<--- Score

50. Cloud native apps, who done done it?

<--- Score

51. What is the best time to involve a migration partner?

<--- Score

52. What Serverless Architectures on AWS skills are most important?

<--- Score

53. How do you audit what you are responsible for?
<--- Score

54. Can different cloud computing service models be mixed?
<--- Score

55. What is your Serverless Architectures on AWS strategy?
<--- Score

56. Who is responsible for ensuring appropriate resources (time, people and money) are allocated to Serverless Architectures on AWS?
<--- Score

57. How can you help ensure the files in your Amazon S3 bucket are secure?
<--- Score

58. How much contingency will be available in the budget?
<--- Score

59. What runs on premises versus in the cloud?
<--- Score

60. Are you maintaining a past–present–future perspective throughout the Serverless Architectures on AWS discussion?
<--- Score

61. How much does Serverless Architectures on AWS

help?

<--- Score

62. What exactly is scaling and why is it important?

<--- Score

63. What are the areas in which serverless architecture has fallen short of expectations?

<--- Score

64. Which other cloud services are you using in conjunction with FaaS?

<--- Score

65. How can you detect if a server has been compromised?

<--- Score

66. What are the most valuable transactions to your customers and to your business?

<--- Score

67. What about resiliency?

<--- Score

68. How is serverless relevant to Ops?

<--- Score

69. How do you assess the Serverless Architectures on AWS pitfalls that are inherent in implementing it?

<--- Score

70. How do you evolve your workload to take advantage of new releases?

<--- Score

71. In the past year, what have you done (or could you have done) to increase the accurate perception of your company/brand as ethical and honest?
<--- Score

72. What is the difference between authentication and authorization?
<--- Score

73. What are the business goals Serverless Architectures on AWS is aiming to achieve?
<--- Score

74. How well can congestion pricing neutralize denial of service attacks?
<--- Score

75. Which packages should be baked into your server images?
<--- Score

76. Have new benefits been realized?
<--- Score

77. What size servers for budget/performance?
<--- Score

78. How was your experience with aws lambda in production?
<--- Score

79. How do you know when you should launch more Amazon EC2 instances?
<--- Score

80. Are new benefits received and understood?

<--- Score

81. How are you building resiliency into your serverless application?
<--- Score

82. Are assumptions made in Serverless Architectures on AWS stated explicitly?
<--- Score

83. What are the benefits of serverless computing?
<--- Score

84. How do you protect your networks?
<--- Score

85. Who do we want your customers to become?
<--- Score

86. In retrospect, of the projects that you pulled the plug on, what percent do you wish had been allowed to keep going, and what percent do you wish had ended earlier?
<--- Score

87. What are the gaps in your knowledge and experience?
<--- Score

88. What about testing?
<--- Score

89. When is service really denied?
<--- Score

90. Do you know the number for how much the

monthly bill was at the end?
<--- Score

91. How do you engage the workforce, in addition to satisfying them?
<--- Score

92. How are you going to be resilient to failures in your topology?
<--- Score

93. Is a Serverless Architectures on AWS team work effort in place?
<--- Score

94. Is your infrastructure well-architected?
<--- Score

95. What size servers are right for your budget?
<--- Score

96. What is the overall talent health of your organization as a whole at senior levels, and for each organization reporting to a member of the Senior Leadership Team?
<--- Score

97. Are you ready for serverless?
<--- Score

98. What is the expected flow of traffic?
<--- Score

99. Have you painted the picture correctly?
<--- Score

100. Code sandboxes: what is the attack surface?
<--- Score

101. Is serverless the future of cloud computing?
<--- Score

102. Why should people listen to you?
<--- Score

103. What are the major advantages and challenges of using serverless and FaaS in practice?
<--- Score

104. How are customers using AWS lambda?
<--- Score

105. What happens at your organization when people fail?
<--- Score

106. Why is Serverless Architectures on AWS important for you now?
<--- Score

107. Are there any activities that you can take off your to do list?
<--- Score

108. What business benefits will Serverless Architectures on AWS goals deliver if achieved?
<--- Score

109. How can you increase utilization of your servers?
<--- Score

110. Why serverless computing?
<--- Score

111. Are the limitations of FaaS actually healthy for the future of distributed programming?
<--- Score

112. What exactly do you mean by scaling?
<--- Score

113. How will the application handle server hardware failure?
<--- Score

114. Unintended behavior, can a function be made to do something unexpected?
<--- Score

115. Is your organization using a serverless architecture?
<--- Score

116. How do you pay for FaaS?
<--- Score

117. Is high availability important for your organization?
<--- Score

118. How should a business know or be able to tell if a third party organization can be trusted?
<--- Score

119. How do you protect your compute resources?
<--- Score

120. If no one would ever find out about your accomplishments, how would you lead differently?
<--- Score

121. Can you use Lambda, Azure Functions, Google Cloud Functions and Apache OpenWhisk in one project?
<--- Score

122. What is the future for IoT in retail fulfilment and logistics?
<--- Score

123. How does serverless make security harder?
<--- Score

124. How do you match supply of resources with demand?
<--- Score

125. Do you consider a deployment method to be permanent ?
<--- Score

126. How do you create buy-in?
<--- Score

127. Do you see serverless architecture as an alternative for future applications?
<--- Score

128. Can cloud power ground-breaking research?
<--- Score

129. What are current Serverless Architectures on AWS

paradigms?
<--- Score

130. When should you choose a serverless architecture over a server-based one?
<--- Score

131. Where can you break convention?
<--- Score

132. What should you stop doing?
<--- Score

133. Do you see serverless as a fad, or do you think it will be here to stay?
<--- Score

134. Which os should your servers run?
<--- Score

135. How much of your infrastructure is actually being used?
<--- Score

136. How will new code be deployed to your servers?
<--- Score

137. What is the future for Dev and Ops teams?
<--- Score

138. How do you foster innovation?
<--- Score

139. How do you determine the key elements that affect Serverless Architectures on AWS workforce

satisfaction, how are these elements determined for different workforce groups and segments?
<--- Score

140. What could happen if you do not do it?
<--- Score

141. What difference does caching make?
<--- Score

142. What are your personal philosophies regarding Serverless Architectures on AWS and how do they influence your work?
<--- Score

143. Which features are particularly suitable to be implemented in which functions?
<--- Score

144. What is the main threat to Serverless Architecture?
<--- Score

145. How have you explored the already stated different compute options when architecting AWS Batch?
<--- Score

146. What does success look like?
<--- Score

147. How to pick the right fast storage size?
<--- Score

148. Does it even matter where it lives?
<--- Score

149. What do we do when new problems arise?
<--- Score

150. How do you use pre-trained models for serving predictions?
<--- Score

151. Have you tested your AWS Lambda function?
<--- Score

152. Do you attempt to get something basic in the beginning?
<--- Score

153. What services have you been using?
<--- Score

154. How are you regulating access rates to and within your serverless application?
<--- Score

155. How does your system withstand component failures?
<--- Score

156. How secure is serverless architecture?
<--- Score

157. Why should applications be restricted to one cloud?
<--- Score

158. How to build serverless apps serverlessly?
<--- Score

159. What can you actively automate to defend ourselves?

<--- Score

160. If your company went out of business tomorrow, would anyone who doesn't get a paycheck here care?

<--- Score

161. How effective do you think the master user record will be?

<--- Score

162. Why make the switch?

<--- Score

163. Why multi-region?

<--- Score

164. How does the software get vetted?

<--- Score

165. What are the barriers to increased Serverless Architectures on AWS production?

<--- Score

166. How much remaining capacity do your servers have?

<--- Score

167. How does your organization go serverless?

<--- Score

168. What is effective Serverless Architectures on AWS?

<--- Score

169. How will you know that the Serverless Architectures on AWS project has been successful?
<--- Score

170. Has implementation been effective in reaching specified objectives so far?
<--- Score

171. What one word do you want to own in the minds of your customers, employees, and partners?
<--- Score

172. How do you manage your network topology?
<--- Score

173. What are the languages that AWS Lambda supports?
<--- Score

174. How long does AWS Lambda keep your idle functions around before a cold start?
<--- Score

175. How do you logically manage the resources that make up your serverless app?
<--- Score

176. How does your system adapt to changes in demand?
<--- Score

177. How do you effectively train staff in such new skills?
<--- Score

178. At what moment would you think; Will I get fired?

<--- Score

179. How do you evolve operations?
<--- Score

180. Why did you choose to go Serverless?
<--- Score

181. How do you know that you are ready to support a workload?
<--- Score

182. How do you deal with Serverless Architectures on AWS changes?
<--- Score

183. How do you increase the value you are getting from such investments?
<--- Score

184. What is the catch?
<--- Score

185. What potential megatrends could make your business model obsolete?
<--- Score

186. What happens if you misconfigure something and remove connectivity?
<--- Score

187. Serverless runtimes; how are they different?
<--- Score

188. What makes this different?
<--- Score

189. Why is serverless such a big topic at the moment?
<--- Score

190. Should you use AWS Lambda or EC2?
<--- Score

191. How does buying and selling software change in a serverless world?
<--- Score

192. What unique value proposition (UVP) do you offer?
<--- Score

193. Hybrid execution: which task on FaaS and which on IaaS?
<--- Score

194. How can you tell if a server has been compromised?
<--- Score

195. What else can be done with AWS lambda?
<--- Score

196. Which programming languages do or did you use with FaaS?
<--- Score

197. Why is serverless a paradigm shift for your business economics?
<--- Score

198. Do you know what you are doing? And who do

you call if you don't?

<--- Score

199. What do other people use serverless for?

<--- Score

200. Evolution of server computing: vms to containers to serverless which to use when?

<--- Score

201. What are the key architectural patterns and best practices for building FaaS applications?

<--- Score

202. What can serverless computing do?

<--- Score

203. What would you ask of the vendor space?

<--- Score

204. How are you implementing asynchronous transactions?

<--- Score

205. How to dispatch tasks to various infrastructures?

<--- Score

206. How do you authorize and authenticate access to your serverless api?

<--- Score

207. When deploying an application do you provision for peak load or implement auto scaling ?

<--- Score

208. What is your strategy on input validation?

<--- Score

209. How would a combined container and serverless architecture look?

<--- Score

210. Can you predict when certain geographies have the greatest demand?

<--- Score

211. Should you go all-in with one managed cloud partner or work with your existing application vendors?

<--- Score

212. Can you automate security testing of serverless?

<--- Score

213. How do you lock down what each function can do?

<--- Score

214. Which Serverless Architectures on AWS goals are the most important?

<--- Score

215. How can you negotiate Serverless Architectures on AWS successfully with a stubborn boss, an irate client, or a deceitful coworker?

<--- Score

216. How do senior leaders deploy your organizations vision and values through your leadership system, to

the workforce, to key suppliers and partners, and to customers and other stakeholders, as appropriate?
<--- Score

217. Do you consider load an important factor when choosing your application stack ?
<--- Score

218. How are you enforcing networking boundaries as to what aws lambda functions can access?
<--- Score

219. Are you a first-time user of AWS lambda?
<--- Score

220. Where does serverless computing apply?
<--- Score

221. If you have your application, which is kind of waiting for something to happen, and its still kind of running, you are still paying for that, right?
<--- Score

222. What is an automatic scaling policy?
<--- Score

223. Where can you persist code?
<--- Score

224. Is migrating to the cloud essentially like moving from one server to another?
<--- Score

225. Who has permission to deploy functions?
<--- Score

226. How long does aws lambda keep your idle functions around?
<--- Score

227. What role does communication play in the success or failure of a Serverless Architectures on AWS project?
<--- Score

228. Why would you adopt a serverless architecture?
<--- Score

229. What about security and hosting and maintenance?
<--- Score

230. What managed services do you choose?
<--- Score

231. Have you considered serverless limits for peak workloads?
<--- Score

232. How many users create too much load for your servers?
<--- Score

233. How do you go about integration testing?
<--- Score

234. How does the Stack apply to IaaS & FaaS?
<--- Score

235. What is the purpose of Serverless Architectures

on AWS in relation to the mission?
<--- Score

236. Is serverless fundamentally stateless?
<--- Score

237. How do you handle server configuration changes?
<--- Score

238. How is serverless computing different from containers?
<--- Score

239. If you use FaaS to implement a REST endpoint or HTTP service, how fine-grained are functions?
<--- Score

240. How does aws lambda run your code?
<--- Score

241. How to deploy an application?
<--- Score

242. Are permissions that your app has what you would expect?
<--- Score

243. Resource selection, which task on which cloud function type?
<--- Score

244. Ultimately, are you going to be at a NoOps state?
<--- Score

245. Why is serverless attractive?
<--- Score

246. Are lambdas limitations fundamental?
<--- Score

247. Distributed cloud market; who benefits from specification flexibilities?
<--- Score

248. Can you do all this work?
<--- Score

249. Does a Serverless Architectures on AWS quantification method exist?
<--- Score

250. How many are familiar with cloud concepts, like IaaS, PaaS, SaaS?
<--- Score

251. What are the models for engaging with OIT and/or cloud vendors?
<--- Score

252. Is your organization using serverless technology?
<--- Score

253. Should you worry about memory loss?
<--- Score

254. If you find that you havent accomplished one of the goals for one of the steps of the Serverless Architectures on AWS strategy, what will you do to fix it?

<--- Score

255. Does infrastructure retention vary throughout the day based on system load?
<--- Score

256. How to do versioning?
<--- Score

257. How do you test resilience?
<--- Score

258. What Is the AWS Serverless Application Repository?
<--- Score

259. Are you really building a serverless system?
<--- Score

260. What is unique about lambda?
<--- Score

261. Access from a function, what can a function access when it is running?
<--- Score

262. What are the potential basics of Serverless Architectures on AWS fraud?
<--- Score

263. Will there be any necessary staff changes (redundancies or new hires)?
<--- Score

264. What stupid rule would you most like to kill?
<--- Score

265. Are you making progress, and are you making progress as Serverless Architectures on AWS leaders?
<--- Score

266. Why will customers want to buy your organizations products/services?
<--- Score

267. What is a good buffer cache replacement scheme for mobile flash storage?
<--- Score

268. How do you use this amount of resources efficiently and effectively across the number of people and the number of jobs that want to run on it?
<--- Score

269. Can the schedule be done in the given time?
<--- Score

270. Will serverless end the dominance of linux in the cloud?
<--- Score

271. Who are the key stakeholders?
<--- Score

272. Where do you see sprawl?
<--- Score

273. How do you make it meaningful in connecting Serverless Architectures on AWS with what users do day-to-day?
<--- Score

274. What is going on inside the network?
<--- Score

275. What do you use FaaS for in the backend?
<--- Score

276. How do you know if you are successful?
<--- Score

277. Think about your organization in ways of was the infrastructure really that expensive?
<--- Score

278. What happens when a new employee joins the organization?
<--- Score

279. How do you implement change?
<--- Score

280. Who do you think the world wants your organization to be?
<--- Score

281. How do you govern usage?
<--- Score

282. Are you familiar with Serverless Functions and Docker containers ?
<--- Score

283. Who/where/when is allowed to execute?
<--- Score

284. How many functions do the FaaS systems or

applications typically consist of?
<--- Score

285. What will you build with Serverless?
<--- Score

286. What happens before the code is deployed?
<--- Score

287. Which approach is better for your organization, containers or AWS Lambda?
<--- Score

288. Can you automate it?
<--- Score

289. What are your desired degrees of quality-of-service?
<--- Score

290. When information truly is ubiquitous, when reach and connectivity are completely global, when computing resources are infinite, and when a whole new set of impossibilities are not only possible, but happening, what will that do to your business?
<--- Score

291. What is the maximum execution time for a Lambda function to run that can be assigned?
<--- Score

292. Since the container is truly ephemeral how do you detect anomalous behavior?
<--- Score

293. Why would you want to self-host the ability

to have a serverless architecture built on top of Kubernetes?
<--- Score

294. What would you recommend your friend do if he/she were facing this dilemma?
<--- Score

295. Why build when someone else might have already done it?
<--- Score

296. How do you manage credentials and authentication?
<--- Score

297. Are blockchain smart contracts serverless?
<--- Score

298. Where did your Serverless journey start?
<--- Score

299. Which approach is better, containers or AWS Lambda?
<--- Score

300. What if you want to roll back?
<--- Score

301. When should you enable the Configure as Proxy Resource option?
<--- Score

302. How do you provide a safe environment -physically and emotionally?
<--- Score

303. What are the success criteria that will indicate that Serverless Architectures on AWS objectives have been met and the benefits delivered?
<--- Score

304. Who should be notified when something goes wrong?
<--- Score

305. Why do you see startups and serverless as a natural match?
<--- Score

306. How are venture capital organizations reacting to serverless?
<--- Score

307. How do you decommission resources?
<--- Score

308. Is it easier to change your infrastructure in the cloud then on premise?
<--- Score

309. How do you accomplish your long range Serverless Architectures on AWS goals?
<--- Score

310. How is cloud computing different from on-premise?
<--- Score

311. What if you want to switch to another model?
<--- Score

312. Will you be able to absorb an attempted Denial of Service (DoS) attack?
<--- Score

313. What times of day, week, month, quarter, or year are your peak times?
<--- Score

314. What will run at the edge?
<--- Score

315. What new services of functionality will be implemented next with Serverless Architectures on AWS ?
<--- Score

316. How much experience do you have with using cloud services, as AWS EC2, Lambda, or Heroku?
<--- Score

317. Are all key stakeholders present at all Structured Walkthroughs?
<--- Score

318. How can you protect what you cannot see?
<--- Score

319. How do you manage your AWS service limits?
<--- Score

320. What amount of cumulative downtime can this workload realistically accumulate in a year?
<--- Score

321. What is the trade-of between simplicity and expressiveness?

<--- Score

322. How does dynamic automatic scaling work?
<--- Score

323. How will you autorecover and deal with failure?
<--- Score

324. How is it different than containers?
<--- Score

325. When should your function execute?
<--- Score

326. What will change with serverless?
<--- Score

327. Who is responsible?
<--- Score

328. How to migrate to effective infrastructure?
<--- Score

329. Can legacy code be made to run serverless?
<--- Score

330. Is the docker daemon running on this host?
<--- Score

331. Can you answer questions as; is this resource accessible by a particular user?
<--- Score

332. Can you use traditional tools?
<--- Score

333. If you were moving to NoOps, how does automation relate to serverless computing, and what do you expect as far as innovations there?
<--- Score

334. What about serverless?
<--- Score

335. How fast is realtime ?
<--- Score

336. How long can you persist code?
<--- Score

337. What are the major advantages that you see in serverless?
<--- Score

338. Have you used a FaaS service in the past?
<--- Score

339. How can you protect what you can not see?
<--- Score

340. Do you feel that more should be done in the Serverless Architectures on AWS area?
<--- Score

341. Do you have an implicit bias for capital investments over people investments?
<--- Score

342. Can you do it?
<--- Score

343. Without a server, how do you authenticate users and secure access to resources?
<--- Score

344. How does proportional cpu allocation work with aws lambda?
<--- Score

345. Access to a function, who or what can modify or invoke a function?
<--- Score

346. How can you answer the really big questions?
<--- Score

347. What are you challenging?
<--- Score

348. What else can you do with AWS Lambda?
<--- Score

349. What is AWS lambda in AWS devops?
<--- Score

350. Do you have experience deploying applications to one of the major cloud platforms ?
<--- Score

351. Why is serverless important to NoOps?
<--- Score

352. How long will it take to change?
<--- Score

353. Is this a read-heavy, write-heavy, or balanced workload?

<--- Score

354. What capabilities does a service mesh provide?
<--- Score

355. How fine-grained pricing can be?
<--- Score

356. Whom among your colleagues do you trust, and for what?
<--- Score

357. How will you ensure you get what you expected?
<--- Score

358. Who can access?
<--- Score

359. What was the last experiment you ran?
<--- Score

360. Is your code architecture running unnecessary lambda functions?
<--- Score

361. How does language, memory and package size affect cold starts of AWS Lambda?
<--- Score

362. How do you respond to an incident?
<--- Score

363. What is your strategy for code logging in your lambda functions?
<--- Score

364. What are you paying, and what for?
<--- Score

365. When should you use aws lambda?
<--- Score

366. Which services are real bottlenecks or resource hogs today?
<--- Score

367. How are you enforcing boundaries as to what aws services your lambda functions can access?
<--- Score

368. Why build this?
<--- Score

369. Can you maintain your growth without detracting from the factors that have contributed to your success?
<--- Score

370. Multi-path streaming: is it worth the trouble?
<--- Score

371. What exactly are you deploying?
<--- Score

372. Is your code architecture running unnecessary lambda functions in order to reduce complexity?
<--- Score

373. How do the Security Features Stack Up?
<--- Score

374. How to enforce safety/security/auditability during production changes?

<--- Score

375. If you got fired and a new hire took your place, what would she do different?

<--- Score

376. What about vendor lock-in?

<--- Score

377. Are you using serverless in your application logic?

<--- Score

378. Too many tools?

<--- Score

379. Were lessons learned captured and communicated?

<--- Score

380. What are the key enablers to make this Serverless Architectures on AWS move?

<--- Score

381. How many people should maintain it?

<--- Score

382. What is a mesh?

<--- Score

383. Where can you use serverless?

<--- Score

384. When should you use AWS Lambda versus Amazon EC2?

<--- Score

385. Which users should have access to your servers?

<--- Score

386. Who has the serverless advantage?

<--- Score

387. Can you explain the rationale for choosing serverless?

<--- Score

Add up total points for this section:
_ _ _ _ _ = Total points for this section

Divided by: _ _ _ _ _ _ (number of statements answered) = _ _ _ _ _ _
Average score for this section

Transfer your score to the Serverless Architectures on AWS Index at the beginning of the Self-Assessment.

Serverless Architectures On AWS and Managing Projects, Criteria for Project Managers:

1.0 Initiating Process Group: Serverless Architectures On AWS

1. For technology Serverless Architectures On AWS projects only: Are all production support stakeholders (Business unit, technical support, & user) prepared for implementation with appropriate contingency plans?

2. Realistic - are the desired results expressed in a way that the team will be motivated and believe that the required level of involvement will be obtained?

3. How is each deliverable reviewed, verified, and validated?

4. What are the pressing issues of the hour?

5. What will you do?

6. Are the changes in your Serverless Architectures On AWS project being formally requested, analyzed, and approved by the appropriate decision makers?

7. How well did you do?

8. Specific - is the objective clear in terms of what, how, when, and where the situation will be changed?

9. Are identified risks being monitored properly, are new risks arising during the Serverless Architectures On AWS project or are foreseen risks occurring?

10. Who is funding the Serverless Architectures On AWS project?

11. How well defined and documented were the Serverless Architectures On AWS project management processes you chose to use?

12. Who is behind the Serverless Architectures On AWS project?

13. When will the Serverless Architectures On AWS project be done?

14. Are the Serverless Architectures On AWS project team and stakeholders meeting regularly and using a meeting agenda and taking notes to accurately document what is being covered and what happened in the weekly meetings?

15. Have the stakeholders identified all individual requirements pertaining to business process?

16. What areas does the group agree are the biggest success on the Serverless Architectures On AWS project?

17. During which stage of Risk planning are risks prioritized based on probability and impact?

18. Did the Serverless Architectures On AWS project team have the right skills?

19. Were resources available as planned?

20. Based on your Serverless Architectures On AWS project communication management plan, what worked well?

1.1 Project Charter: Serverless Architectures On AWS

21. Who is the sponsor?

22. How do you manage integration?

23. Why do you manage integration?

24. Fit with other Products Compliments – Cannibalizes?

25. What date will the task finish?

26. What does it need to do?

27. What material?

28. Why is a Serverless Architectures On AWS project Charter used?

29. What are the assigned resources?

30. How will you know that a change is an improvement?

31. Strategic fit: what is the strategic initiative identifier for this Serverless Architectures On AWS project?

32. Why Outsource?

33. Where and how does the team fit within your

organization structure?

34. Why is it important?

35. Why do you need to manage scope?

36. When is a charter needed?

37. Who is the Serverless Architectures On AWS project Manager?

38. Market – identify products market, including whether it is outside of the objective: what is the purpose of the program or Serverless Architectures On AWS project?

39. What are some examples of a business case?

40. How much?

1.2 Stakeholder Register: Serverless Architectures On AWS

41. Who is managing stakeholder engagement?

42. What opportunities exist to provide communications?

43. How much influence do they have on the Serverless Architectures On AWS project?

44. What is the power of the stakeholder?

45. Who are the stakeholders?

46. What are the major Serverless Architectures On AWS project milestones requiring communications or providing communications opportunities?

47. How should employers make voices heard?

48. How big is the gap?

49. Is your organization ready for change?

50. Who wants to talk about Security?

51. How will reports be created?

52. What & Why?

1.3 Stakeholder Analysis Matrix: Serverless Architectures On AWS

53. What are the key services, contractual arrangements, or other relationships between stakeholder groups?

54. What is your organizations competitors doing?

55. Vulnerable groups; who are the vulnerable groups that might be affected by the Serverless Architectures On AWS project?

56. Lack of competitive strength?

57. How can you counter negative efforts?

58. Environmental effects?

59. Are they likely to influence the success or failure of your Serverless Architectures On AWS project?

60. How do they affect the Serverless Architectures On AWS project and its outcomes?

61. Could any of your organizations weaknesses seriously threaten development?

62. What do your organizations stakeholders do better than anyone else?

63. Is there a clear description of the scope of practice of the Serverless Architectures On AWS projects

educators?

64. What is the issue at stake?

65. Resource providers; who can provide resources to ensure the implementation of the Serverless Architectures On AWS project?

66. Opponents; who are the opponents?

67. Accreditations, etc?

68. Why is it important to identify them?

69. Processes and systems, etc?

70. What coalitions might build around the issues being tackled?

71. Tactics: eg, surprise, major contracts?

72. Who will be affected by the Serverless Architectures On AWS project?

2.0 Planning Process Group: Serverless Architectures On AWS

73. What factors are contributing to progress or delay in the achievement of products and results?

74. What is involved in Serverless Architectures On AWS project scope management, and why is good Serverless Architectures On AWS project scope management so important on information technology Serverless Architectures On AWS projects?

75. How does activity resource estimation affect activity duration estimation?

76. In which Serverless Architectures On AWS project management process group is the detailed Serverless Architectures On AWS project budget created?

77. Professionals want to know what is expected from them; what are the deliverables?

78. What is the NEXT thing to do?

79. Are there efficient coordination mechanisms to avoid overloading the counterparts, participating stakeholders?

80. If you are late, will anybody notice?

81. What makes your Serverless Architectures On AWS project successful?

82. In what way has the Serverless Architectures On AWS project come up with innovative measures for problem-solving?

83. Have more efficient (sensitive) and appropriate measures been adopted to respond to the political and socio-cultural problems identified?

84. Product breakdown structure (pbs): what is the Serverless Architectures On AWS project result or product, and how should it look like, what are its parts?

85. Why is it important to determine activity sequencing on Serverless Architectures On AWS projects?

86. How well defined and documented are the Serverless Architectures On AWS project management processes you chose to use?

87. If task x starts two days late, what is the effect on the Serverless Architectures On AWS project end date?

88. To what extent has a PMO contributed to raising the quality of the design of the Serverless Architectures On AWS project?

89. If action is called for, what form should it take?

90. Have operating capacities been created and/or reinforced in partners?

91. What is the critical path for this Serverless Architectures On AWS project, and what is the

duration of the critical path?

92. To what extent has the intervention strategy been adapted to the areas of intervention in which it is being implemented?

2.1 Project Management Plan: Serverless Architectures On AWS

93. Are there any Client staffing expectations?

94. Are the proposed Serverless Architectures On AWS project purposes different than a previously authorized Serverless Architectures On AWS project?

95. Is the budget realistic?

96. What does management expect of PMs?

97. Was the peer (technical) review of the cost estimates duly coordinated with the cost estimate center of expertise and addressed in the review documentation and certification?

98. Who manages integration?

99. Development trends and opportunities. What if the positive direction and vision of your organization causes expected trends to change?

100. What would you do differently what did not work?

101. What went wrong?

102. Are there non-structural buyout or relocation recommendations?

103. Did the planning effort collaborate to develop

solutions that integrate expertise, policies, programs, and Serverless Architectures On AWS projects across entities?

104. When is the Serverless Architectures On AWS project management plan created?

105. What worked well?

106. Is there an incremental analysis/cost effectiveness analysis of proposed mitigation features based on an approved method and using an accepted model?

107. Is mitigation authorized or recommended?

108. If the Serverless Architectures On AWS project management plan is a comprehensive document that guides you in Serverless Architectures On AWS project execution and control, then what should it NOT contain?

109. What data/reports/tools/etc. do program managers need?

110. Are there any windfall benefits that would accrue to the Serverless Architectures On AWS project sponsor or other parties?

111. How do you manage time?

2.2 Scope Management Plan: Serverless Architectures On AWS

112. Are alternatives safe, functional, constructible, economical, reasonable and sustainable?

113. Are the Serverless Architectures On AWS project team members located locally to the users/ stakeholders?

114. Pop quiz – what changed on Serverless Architectures On AWS project scope statement input?

115. How much money have you spent?

116. Are there any scope changes proposed for the previously authorized Serverless Architectures On AWS project?

117. How will scope changes be identified and classified?

118. Is the communication plan being followed?

119. Are the budget estimates reasonable?

120. What do you need to do to accomplish the goal or goals?

121. Has a capability assessment been conducted?

122. Are risk triggers captured?

123. Can the Serverless Architectures On AWS project team do several activities in parallel?

124. Have adequate procedures been put in place for Serverless Architectures On AWS project communication and status reporting across Serverless Architectures On AWS project boundaries (for example interdependent software development among interfacing systems)?

125. Have the personnel with the necessary skills and competence been identified and has agreement for participation in the Serverless Architectures On AWS project been reached with the appropriate management?

126. Time estimation – how much time will be needed?

127. Does the detailed work plan match the complexity of tasks with the capabilities of personnel?

128. Are measurements and feedback mechanisms incorporated in tracking work effort & refining work estimating techniques?

129. Is there a formal process for updating the Serverless Architectures On AWS project baseline?

130. Process groups – where do scope management processes fit in?

131. What threats might prevent you from getting there?

2.3 Requirements Management Plan: Serverless Architectures On AWS

132. How do you know that you have done this right?

133. Controlling Serverless Architectures On AWS project requirements involves monitoring the status of the Serverless Architectures On AWS project requirements and managing changes to the requirements. Who is responsible for monitoring and tracking the Serverless Architectures On AWS project requirements?

134. How will you communicate scheduled tasks to other team members?

135. Who is responsible for monitoring and tracking the Serverless Architectures On AWS project requirements?

136. What is the earliest finish date for this Serverless Architectures On AWS project if it is scheduled to start on ...?

137. Will the product release be stable and mature enough to be deployed in the user community?

138. How will unresolved questions be handled once approval has been obtained?

139. Who is responsible for quantifying the Serverless Architectures On AWS project requirements?

140. Who will perform the analysis?

141. Will you use an assessment of the Serverless Architectures On AWS project environment as a tool to discover risk to the requirements process?

142. What information regarding the Serverless Architectures On AWS project requirements will be reported?

143. Will the Serverless Architectures On AWS project requirements become approved in writing?

144. Is there formal agreement on who has authority to request a change in requirements?

145. Will you perform a Requirements Risk assessment and develop a plan to deal with risks?

146. Is the system software (non-operating system) new to the IT Serverless Architectures On AWS project team?

147. Do you have price sheets and a methodology for determining the total proposal cost?

148. How will you develop the schedule of requirements activities?

149. Are all the stakeholders ready for the transition into the user community?

150. What are you trying to do?

2.4 Requirements Documentation: Serverless Architectures On AWS

151. What is effective documentation?

152. Can the requirements be checked?

153. Do technical resources exist?

154. Who provides requirements?

155. Validity. does the system provide the functions which best support the customers needs?

156. What are current process problems?

157. What can tools do for us?

158. Who is interacting with the system?

159. Consistency. are there any requirements conflicts?

160. What are the potential disadvantages/ advantages?

161. What marketing channels do you want to use: e-mail, letter or sms?

162. Where do you define what is a customer, what are the attributes of customer?

163. If applicable; are there issues linked with the fact

that this is an offshore Serverless Architectures On AWS project?

164. Verifiability. can the requirements be checked?

165. How will they be documented / shared?

166. Have the benefits identified with the system being identified clearly?

167. How to document system requirements?

168. What if the system wasn t implemented?

169. How linear / iterative is your Requirements Gathering process (or will it be)?

2.5 Requirements Traceability Matrix: Serverless Architectures On AWS

170. Why do you manage scope?

171. Is there a requirements traceability process in place?

172. Will you use a Requirements Traceability Matrix?

173. What is the WBS?

174. How will it affect the stakeholders personally in career?

175. Why use a WBS?

176. What percentage of Serverless Architectures On AWS projects are producing traceability matrices between requirements and other work products?

177. Describe the process for approving requirements so they can be added to the traceability matrix and Serverless Architectures On AWS project work can be performed. Will the Serverless Architectures On AWS project requirements become approved in writing?

178. How do you manage scope?

179. Do you have a clear understanding of all subcontracts in place?

180. How small is small enough?

181. What are the chronologies, contingencies, consequences, criteria?

2.6 Project Scope Statement: Serverless Architectures On AWS

182. Were potential customers involved early in the planning process?

183. Have the configuration management functions been assigned?

184. Has the format for tracking and monitoring schedules and costs been defined?

185. Do you anticipate new stakeholders joining the Serverless Architectures On AWS project over time?

186. What went right?

187. Is there a Change Management Board?

188. What should you drop in order to add something new?

189. Any new risks introduced or old risks impacted. Are there issues that could affect the existing requirements for the result, service, or product if the scope changes?

190. How often will scope changes be reviewed?

191. What are the major deliverables of the Serverless Architectures On AWS project?

192. Is the plan under configuration management?

193. Is the Serverless Architectures On AWS project sponsor function identified and defined?

194. Is this process communicated to the customer and team members?

195. Who will you recommend approve the change, and when do you recommend the change reviews occur?

196. Are there issues that could affect the existing requirements for the result, service, or product if the scope changes?

197. Are there adequate Serverless Architectures On AWS project control systems?

198. If there are vendors, have they signed off on the Serverless Architectures On AWS project Plan?

199. Will an issue form be in use?

200. Is the quality function identified and assigned?

201. Is there a Quality Assurance Plan documented and filed?

2.7 Assumption and Constraint Log: Serverless Architectures On AWS

202. How can you prevent/fix violations?

203. Have Serverless Architectures On AWS project management standards and procedures been established and documented?

204. How many Serverless Architectures On AWS project staff does this specific process affect?

205. What would you gain if you spent time working to improve this process?

206. How can constraints be violated?

207. Are there procedures in place to effectively manage interdependencies with other Serverless Architectures On AWS projects / systems?

208. Does the system design reflect the requirements?

209. What strengths do you have?

210. Have adequate resources been provided by management to ensure Serverless Architectures On AWS project success?

211. Is this model reasonable?

212. After observing execution of process, is it in compliance with the documented Plan?

213. Do documented requirements exist for all critical components and areas, including technical, business, interfaces, performance, security and conversion requirements?

214. Has a Serverless Architectures On AWS project Communications Plan been developed?

215. Are there processes in place to ensure that all the terms and code concepts have been documented consistently?

216. When can log be discarded?

217. Have all involved stakeholders and work groups committed to the Serverless Architectures On AWS project?

218. How are new requirements or changes to requirements identified?

219. Is the process working, and people are not executing in compliance of the process?

220. What is positive about the current process?

2.8 Work Breakdown Structure: Serverless Architectures On AWS

221. Why is it useful?

222. How many levels?

223. Do you need another level?

224. How will you and your Serverless Architectures On AWS project team define the Serverless Architectures On AWS projects scope and work breakdown structure?

225. What is the probability that the Serverless Architectures On AWS project duration will exceed xx weeks?

226. When does it have to be done?

227. What has to be done?

228. How much detail?

229. Where does it take place?

230. Is it still viable?

231. Who has to do it?

232. When would you develop a Work Breakdown Structure?

233. Can you make it?

234. Why would you develop a Work Breakdown Structure?

235. How big is a work-package?

236. When do you stop?

237. How far down?

238. Is the work breakdown structure (wbs) defined and is the scope of the Serverless Architectures On AWS project clear with assigned deliverable owners?

2.9 WBS Dictionary: Serverless Architectures On AWS

239. Are data being used by managers in an effective manner to ascertain Serverless Architectures On AWS project or functional status, to identify reasons or significant variance, and to initiate appropriate corrective action?

240. Identify potential or actual budget-based and time-based schedule variances?

241. Are budgets or values assigned to work packages and planning packages in terms of dollars, hours, or other measurable units?

242. Is budgeted cost for work performed calculated in a manner consistent with the way work is planned?

243. Should you include sub-activities?

244. All cwbs elements specified for external reporting?

245. Are detailed work packages planned as far in advance as practicable?

246. Does the cost accumulation system provide for summarization of indirect costs from the point of allocation to the contract total?

247. Are the bases and rates for allocating costs from each indirect pool consistently applied?

248. Are estimates of costs at completion generated in a rational, consistent manner?

249. Wbs elements contractually specified for reporting of status to you (lowest level only)?

250. Where engineering standards or other internal work measurement systems are used, is there a formal relationship between corresponding values and work package budgets?

251. Changes in the nature of the overhead requirements?

252. Are time-phased budgets established for planning and control of level of effort activity by category of resource; for example, type of manpower and/or material?

253. Are estimates developed by Serverless Architectures On AWS project personnel coordinated with the already stated responsible for overall management to determine whether required resources will be available according to revised planning?

254. Is cost performance measurement at the point in time most suitable for the category of material involved, and no earlier than the time of actual receipt of material?

255. Appropriate work authorization documents which subdivide the contractual effort and responsibilities, within functional organizations?

2.10 Schedule Management Plan: Serverless Architectures On AWS

256. Are vendor contract reports, reviews and visits conducted periodically?

257. Is there a requirements change management processes in place?

258. Sensitivity analysis?

259. What does a valid Schedule look like?

260. What will be the format of the schedule model?

261. Have all necessary approvals been obtained?

262. Goal: is the schedule feasible and at what cost?

263. Is an industry recognized mechanized support tool(s) being used for Serverless Architectures On AWS project scheduling & tracking?

264. Is a pmo (Serverless Architectures On AWS project management office) in place and provide oversight to the Serverless Architectures On AWS project?

265. Has the ims been resource-loaded and are assigned resources reasonable and available?

266. Are the processes for schedule assessment and analysis defined?

267. Are the activity durations realistic and at an appropriate level of detail for effective management?

268. Have all documents been archived in a Serverless Architectures On AWS project repository for each release?

269. Must the Serverless Architectures On AWS project be complete by a specified date?

270. Do Serverless Architectures On AWS project managers participating in the Serverless Architectures On AWS project know the Serverless Architectures On AWS projects true status first hand?

271. Are all resource assumptions documented?

272. Are enough systems & user personnel assigned to the Serverless Architectures On AWS project?

273. Is there a Steering Committee in place?

274. Where is the scheduling tool and who has access to it to view it?

2.11 Activity List: Serverless Architectures On AWS

275. When will the work be performed?

276. Where will it be performed?

277. What went well?

278. What will be performed?

279. How difficult will it be to do specific activities on this Serverless Architectures On AWS project?

280. How should ongoing costs be monitored to try to keep the Serverless Architectures On AWS project within budget?

281. Who will perform the work?

282. Is infrastructure setup part of your Serverless Architectures On AWS project?

283. What is your organizations history in doing similar activities?

284. In what sequence?

285. How can the Serverless Architectures On AWS project be displayed graphically to better visualize the activities?

286. The wbs is developed as part of a joint planning

session. and how do you know that youhave done this right?

287. For other activities, how much delay can be tolerated?

288. Is there anything planned that does not need to be here?

289. When do the individual activities need to start and finish?

290. What is the probability the Serverless Architectures On AWS project can be completed in xx weeks?

291. What is the total time required to complete the Serverless Architectures On AWS project if no delays occur?

292. How will it be performed?

293. What are you counting on?

2.12 Activity Attributes: Serverless Architectures On AWS

294. Have constraints been applied to the start and finish milestones for the phases?

295. Has management defined a definite timeframe for the turnaround or Serverless Architectures On AWS project window?

296. Were there other ways you could have organized the data to achieve similar results?

297. Resource is assigned to?

298. Does your organization of the data change its meaning?

299. How difficult will it be to complete specific activities on this Serverless Architectures On AWS project?

300. Do you feel very comfortable with your prediction?

301. Resources to accomplish the work?

302. How many days do you need to complete the work scope with a limit of X number of resources?

303. How else could the items be grouped?

304. Are the required resources available or need to

be acquired?

305. What is the general pattern here?

306. Can more resources be added?

307. Time for overtime?

308. Can you re-assign any activities to another resource to resolve an over-allocation?

309. What is missing?

310. Activity: what is In the Bag?

2.13 Milestone List: Serverless Architectures On AWS

311. Political effects?

312. Gaps in capabilities?

313. How late can the activity finish?

314. Effects on core activities, distraction?

315. What background experience, skills, and strengths does the team bring to your organization?

316. Information and research?

317. What are your competitors vulnerabilities?

318. Describe the concept of the technology, product or service that will be or has been developed. How will it be used?

319. Global influences?

320. How will you get the word out to customers?

321. Describe the industry you are in and the market growth opportunities. What is the market for your technology, product or service?

322. New USPs?

323. Vital contracts and partners?

324. What specific improvements did you make to the Serverless Architectures On AWS project proposal since the previous time?

325. Do you foresee any technical risks or developmental challenges?

326. Own known vulnerabilities?

327. What would happen if a delivery of material was one week late?

328. Level of the Innovation?

329. How soon can the activity finish?

2.14 Network Diagram: Serverless Architectures On AWS

330. What is the probability of completing the Serverless Architectures On AWS project in less that xx days?

331. Exercise: what is the probability that the Serverless Architectures On AWS project duration will exceed xx weeks?

332. What activity must be completed immediately before this activity can start?

333. What must be completed before an activity can be started?

334. What job or jobs follow it?

335. Are you on time?

336. Review the logical flow of the network diagram. Take a look at which activities you have first and then sequence the activities. Do they make sense?

337. What is the completion time?

338. Are the required resources available?

339. What controls the start and finish of a job?

340. What activities must follow this activity?

341. What job or jobs could run concurrently?

342. What can be done concurrently?

343. If the Serverless Architectures On AWS project network diagram cannot change and you have extra personnel resources, what is the BEST thing to do?

344. How difficult will it be to do specific activities on this Serverless Architectures On AWS project?

345. Where do you schedule uncertainty time?

346. What are the Major Administrative Issues?

2.15 Activity Resource Requirements: Serverless Architectures On AWS

347. When does monitoring begin?

348. What is the Work Plan Standard?

349. Which logical relationship does the PDM use most often?

350. What are constraints that you might find during the Human Resource Planning process?

351. Anything else?

352. Why do you do that?

353. How do you handle petty cash?

354. Do you use tools like decomposition and rolling-wave planning to produce the activity list and other outputs?

355. Other support in specific areas?

356. Are there unresolved issues that need to be addressed?

357. How many signatures do you require on a check and does this match what is in your policy and procedures?

358. Organizational Applicability?

2.16 Resource Breakdown Structure: Serverless Architectures On AWS

359. What defines a successful Serverless Architectures On AWS project?

360. When do they need the information?

361. The list could probably go on, but, the thing that you would most like to know is, How long & How much?

362. How should the information be delivered?

363. Which resources should be in the resource pool?

364. Goals for the Serverless Architectures On AWS project. What is each stakeholders desired outcome for the Serverless Architectures On AWS project?

365. Who is allowed to see what data about which resources?

366. What is the number one predictor of a groups productivity?

367. What is Serverless Architectures On AWS project communication management?

368. What can you do to improve productivity?

369. What is each stakeholders desired outcome for the Serverless Architectures On AWS project?

370. Who will be used as a Serverless Architectures On AWS project team member?

371. Any changes from stakeholders?

372. How difficult will it be to do specific activities on this Serverless Architectures On AWS project?

373. Who is allowed to perform which functions?

374. What is the difference between % Complete and % work?

2.17 Activity Duration Estimates: Serverless Architectures On AWS

375. Why is there a new or renewed interest in the field of Serverless Architectures On AWS project management?

376. Are updates on work results collected and used as inputs to the performance reporting process?

377. Do procedures exist describing how the Serverless Architectures On AWS project scope will be managed?

378. Briefly describe some key events in the history of Serverless Architectures On AWS project management. What Serverless Architectures On AWS project was the first to use modern Serverless Architectures On AWS project management?

379. Why should Serverless Architectures On AWS project managers strive to make jobs look easy?

380. Account for the make-or-buy process and how to perform the financial calculations involved in the process. What are the main types of contracts if you do decide to outsource?

381. How can software assist in Serverless Architectures On AWS project communications?

382. Does a process exist to identify individuals authorized to make certain decisions?

383. Why is it difficult to use Serverless Architectures On AWS project management software well?

384. What functions does this software provide that cannot be done easily using other tools such as a spreadsheet or database?

385. What is the BEST thing for the Serverless Architectures On AWS project manager to do?

386. Consider the history of modern quality management. How have experts such as Deming, Juran, Crosby, and Taguchi affected the quality movement and todays use of Six Sigma?

387. Total slack can be calculated by which equations?

388. What are the main processes included in Serverless Architectures On AWS project quality management?

389. How have experts such as Deming, Juran, Crosby, and Taguchi affected the quality movement and todays use of Six Sigma?

390. Is a formal written notice that the contract is complete provided to the seller?

391. What are crucial elements of successful Serverless Architectures On AWS project plan execution?

392. Are contingency plans created to prepare for risk events to occur?

393. What are key inputs and outputs of the software?

394. Are Serverless Architectures On AWS project costs tracked in the general ledger?

2.18 Duration Estimating Worksheet: Serverless Architectures On AWS

395. When does your organization expect to be able to complete it?

396. What are the critical bottleneck activities?

397. How should ongoing costs be monitored to try to keep the Serverless Architectures On AWS project within budget?

398. What work will be included in the Serverless Architectures On AWS project?

399. What is next?

400. What is your role?

401. Small or large Serverless Architectures On AWS project?

402. When, then?

403. Define the work as completely as possible. What work will be included in the Serverless Architectures On AWS project?

404. Why estimate time and cost?

405. Do any colleagues have experience with your organization and/or RFPs?

406. Will the Serverless Architectures On AWS project collaborate with the local community and leverage resources?

407. What info is needed?

408. Done before proceeding with this activity or what can be done concurrently?

409. What utility impacts are there?

410. Can the Serverless Architectures On AWS project be constructed as planned?

411. What is cost and Serverless Architectures On AWS project cost management?

412. What is the total time required to complete the Serverless Architectures On AWS project if no delays occur?

2.19 Project Schedule: Serverless Architectures On AWS

413. Schedule/cost recovery?

414. Month Serverless Architectures On AWS project take?

415. To what degree is do you feel the entire team was committed to the Serverless Architectures On AWS project schedule?

416. Have all Serverless Architectures On AWS project delays been adequately accounted for, communicated to all stakeholders and adjustments made in overall Serverless Architectures On AWS project schedule?

417. What is risk?

418. Change management required?

419. Should you have a test for each code module?

420. How detailed should a Serverless Architectures On AWS project get?

421. It allows the Serverless Architectures On AWS project to be delivered on schedule. How Do you Use Schedules?

422. Are activities connected because logic dictates the order in which others occur?

423. Serverless Architectures On AWS project work estimates Who is managing the work estimate quality of work tasks in the Serverless Architectures On AWS project schedule?

424. Meet requirements?

425. What does that mean?

426. How can you minimize or control changes to Serverless Architectures On AWS project schedules?

427. Is infrastructure setup part of your Serverless Architectures On AWS project?

428. Why or why not?

429. How can slack be negative?

430. Why time management?

2.20 Cost Management Plan: Serverless Architectures On AWS

431. Do Serverless Architectures On AWS project teams & team members report on status / activities / progress?

432. Is the structure for tracking the Serverless Architectures On AWS project schedule well defined and assigned to a specific individual?

433. Quality assurance overheads?

434. Serverless Architectures On AWS project definition & scope?

435. Were Serverless Architectures On AWS project team members involved in detailed estimating and scheduling?

436. Has a provision been made to reassess Serverless Architectures On AWS project risks at various Serverless Architectures On AWS project stages?

437. How difficult will it be to do specific tasks on the Serverless Architectures On AWS project?

438. Are adequate resources provided for the quality assurance function?

439. Are changes in scope (deliverable commitments) agreed to by all affected groups & individuals?

440. Schedule contingency – how will the schedule contingency be administrated?

441. Cost / benefit analysis?

442. Are risk oriented checklists used during risk identification?

443. Is current scope of the Serverless Architectures On AWS project substantially different than that originally defined?

444. Are multiple estimation methods being employed?

445. Does the Serverless Architectures On AWS project have a Statement of Work?

446. If you sold 10x widgets on a day, what would the affect on costs be?

447. Have activity relationships and interdependencies within tasks been adequately identified?

448. Do all stakeholders know how to access this repository and where to find the Serverless Architectures On AWS project documentation?

449. Have all team members been part of identifying risks?

2.21 Activity Cost Estimates: Serverless Architectures On AWS

450. What is the estimators estimating history?

451. Review – what are some common errors in activities to avoid?

452. What is the activity inventory?

453. How many activities should you have?

454. Performance bond should always provide what part of the contract value?

455. What were things that you did very well and want to do the same again on the next Serverless Architectures On AWS project?

456. Were you satisfied with the work?

457. What makes a good activity description?

458. Which contract type places the most risk on the seller?

459. Does the estimator estimate by task or by person?

460. What is procurement?

461. Vac -variance at completion, how much over/ under budget do you expect to be?

462. What is a Serverless Architectures On AWS project Management Plan?

463. Was the consultant knowledgeable about the program?

464. What procedures are put in place regarding bidding and cost comparisons, if any?

465. Does the activity use a common approach or business function to deliver its results?

466. Why do you manage cost?

467. Who determines when the contractor is paid?

468. In which phase of the acquisition process cycle does source qualifications reside?

2.22 Cost Estimating Worksheet: Serverless Architectures On AWS

469. What will others want?

470. What costs are to be estimated?

471. Does the Serverless Architectures On AWS project provide innovative ways for stakeholders to overcome obstacles or deliver better outcomes?

472. Identify the timeframe necessary to monitor progress and collect data to determine how the selected measure has changed?

473. Who is best positioned to know and assist in identifying corresponding factors?

474. Will the Serverless Architectures On AWS project collaborate with the local community and leverage resources?

475. What can be included?

476. Value pocket identification & quantification what are value pockets?

477. What additional Serverless Architectures On AWS project(s) could be initiated as a result of this Serverless Architectures On AWS project?

478. Is the Serverless Architectures On AWS project responsive to community need?

479. What is the purpose of estimating?

480. Can a trend be established from historical performance data on the selected measure and are the criteria for using trend analysis or forecasting methods met?

481. Is it feasible to establish a control group arrangement?

482. How will the results be shared and to whom?

483. What happens to any remaining funds not used?

484. Ask: are others positioned to know, are others credible, and will others cooperate?

485. What is the estimated labor cost today based upon this information?

2.23 Cost Baseline: Serverless Architectures On AWS

486. What would the life cycle costs be?

487. Is there anything unique in this Serverless Architectures On AWS projects scope statement that will affect resources?

488. How accurate do cost estimates need to be?

489. Has the Serverless Architectures On AWS project documentation been archived or otherwise disposed as described in the Serverless Architectures On AWS project communication plan?

490. How concrete were original objectives?

491. Impact to environment?

492. What can go wrong?

493. Who will use corresponding metrics ?

494. What is your organizations history in doing similar tasks?

495. Definition of done can be traced back to the definitions of what are you providing to the customer in terms of deliverables?

496. Does it impact schedule, cost, quality?

497. How likely is it to go wrong?

498. How difficult will it be to do specific tasks on the Serverless Architectures On AWS project?

499. Does the suggested change request represent a desired enhancement to the products functionality?

500. Escalation criteria met?

501. What deliverables come first?

502. Has the appropriate access to relevant data and analysis capability been granted?

2.24 Quality Management Plan: Serverless Architectures On AWS

503. What data do you gather/use/compile?

504. Who else should be involved ?

505. Do you keep back-up copies of any data?

506. Who is responsible for approving the qapp?

507. Have all stakeholders been identified?

508. What are your results for key measures/indicators of accomplishment of organizational strategy?

509. Sampling part of task?

510. How do senior leaders create an environment that encourages learning and innovation?

511. How does your organization design processes to ensure others meet customer and others requirements?

512. Does the program conduct field testing?

513. How does your organization manage work to promote cooperation, individual initiative, innovation, flexibility, communications, and knowledge/skill sharing across work units?

514. Is this process still needed?

515. Where do you focus?

516. Would impacts defined serve as impediments?

517. Have all involved stakeholders and work groups committed to the Serverless Architectures On AWS project?

518. Who needs a qmp?

519. What type of in-house testing do you conduct?

520. How do you check in-coming sample material?

521. What is the Difference Between a QMP and QAPP?

522. What methods are used?

2.25 Quality Metrics: Serverless Architectures On AWS

523. How can the effectiveness of each of the activities be measured?

524. The metrics—what is being considered?

525. Which are the right metrics to use?

526. Have risk areas been identified?

527. Where did complaints, returns and warranty claims come from?

528. When will the Final Guidance will be issued?

529. Do the operators focus on determining; is there anything you need to worry about?

530. Product Availability ?

531. What are your organizations next steps?

532. Are quality metrics defined?

533. What about still open problems?

534. Filter visualizations of interest?

535. Are there any open risk issues?

536. What metrics do you measure?

537. What documentation is required?

538. Can visual measures help you to filter visualizations of interest?

539. What is the benchmark?

540. What method of measurement do you use?

541. Do you stratify metrics by product or site?

542. What percentage are outcome-based?

2.26 Process Improvement Plan: Serverless Architectures On AWS

543. Are you following the quality standards?

544. Why do you want to achieve the goal?

545. If a process improvement framework is being used, which elements will help the problems and goals listed?

546. What personnel are the change agents for your initiative?

547. Why quality management?

548. Have storage and access mechanisms and procedures been determined?

549. To elicit goal statements, do you ask a question such as, What do you want to achieve?

550. Who should prepare the process improvement action plan?

551. What personnel are the champions for the initiative?

552. Does your process ensure quality?

553. Modeling current processes is great, and will you ever see a return on that investment?

554. Purpose of goal: the motive is determined by asking, why do you want to achieve this goal?

555. Are there forms and procedures to collect and record the data?

556. Are you meeting the quality standards?

557. The motive is determined by asking, Why do you want to achieve this goal?

558. Where do you want to be?

559. What personnel are the coaches for your initiative?

560. What makes people good SPI coaches?

2.27 Responsibility Assignment Matrix: Serverless Architectures On AWS

561. Budgets assigned to major functional organizations?

562. Budgeted cost for work scheduled?

563. Is it safe to say you can handle more work or that some tasks you are supposed to do arent worth doing?

564. What are the known stakeholder requirements?

565. No rs: if a task has no one listed as responsible, who is getting the job done?

566. Are records maintained to show how undistributed budgets are controlled?

567. What do people write/say on status/Serverless Architectures On AWS project reports?

568. Are the actual costs used for variance analysis reconcilable with data from the accounting system?

569. Are data elements reconcilable between internal summary reports and reports forwarded to stakeholders?

570. Serverless Architectures On AWS projected economic escalation?

571. Incurrence of actual indirect costs in excess of budgets, by element of expense?

572. Are people afraid to let you know when others are under allocated?

573. How do you assist them to be as productive as possible?

574. Will too many Signing-off responsibilities delay the completion of the activity/deliverable?

575. What are the constraints?

576. Where does all this information come from?

577. Changes in the direct base to which overhead costs are allocated?

578. Evaluate the performance of operating organizations?

579. The already stated responsible for overhead performance control of related costs?

2.28 Roles and Responsibilities: Serverless Architectures On AWS

580. Do the values and practices inherent in the culture of your organization foster or hinder the process?

581. What is working well within your organizations performance management system?

582. What specific behaviors did you observe?

583. What should you do now to ensure that you are exceeding expectations and excelling in your current position?

584. Influence: what areas of organizational decision making are you able to influence when you do not have authority to make the final decision?

585. Was the expectation clearly communicated?

586. Implementation of actions: Who are the responsible units?

587. Is there a training program in place for stakeholders covering expectations, roles and responsibilities and any addition knowledge others need to be good stakeholders?

588. Are your budgets supportive of a culture of quality data?

589. What should you highlight for improvement?

590. Key conclusions and recommendations: Are conclusions and recommendations relevant and acceptable?

591. Is feedback clearly communicated and non-judgmental?

592. What expectations were NOT met?

593. What should you do now to prepare yourself for a promotion, increased responsibilities or a different job?

594. Does your vision/mission support a culture of quality data?

595. Are governance roles and responsibilities documented?

596. Accountabilities: what are the roles and responsibilities of individual team members?

597. Where are you most strong as a supervisor?

598. What areas of supervision are challenging for you?

599. What are your major roles and responsibilities in the area of performance measurement and assessment?

2.29 Human Resource Management Plan: Serverless Architectures On AWS

600. Have external dependencies been captured in the schedule?

601. Is the structure for tracking the Serverless Architectures On AWS project schedule well defined and assigned to a specific individual?

602. Does the resource management plan include a personnel development plan?

603. Has a quality assurance plan been developed for the Serverless Architectures On AWS project?

604. Is your organization human?

605. Is a payment system in place with proper reviews and approvals?

606. What communication items need improvement?

607. Who is evaluated?

608. Have the procedures for identifying budget variances been followed?

609. Is a stakeholder management plan in place that covers topics?

610. Was the scope definition used in task sequencing?

611. How are superior performers differentiated from average performers?

612. Are there dependencies with other initiatives or Serverless Architectures On AWS projects?

613. Do Serverless Architectures On AWS project managers participating in the Serverless Architectures On AWS project know the Serverless Architectures On AWS projects true status first hand?

614. Has the Serverless Architectures On AWS project scope been baselined?

615. Are tasks tracked by hours?

616. Staffing Requirements?

617. Are all payments made according to the contract(s)?

2.30 Communications Management Plan: Serverless Architectures On AWS

618. Who is responsible?

619. Which team member will work with each stakeholder?

620. Timing: when do the effects of the communication take place?

621. What is the stakeholders level of authority?

622. Do you then often overlook a key stakeholder or stakeholder group?

623. Do you feel more overwhelmed by stakeholders?

624. Are others part of the communications management plan?

625. What help do you and your team need from the stakeholder?

626. How do you manage communications?

627. What to learn?

628. Who to learn from?

629. What data is going to be required?

630. How much time does it take to do it?

631. Who are the members of the governing body?

632. Do you feel a register helps?

633. Which stakeholders can influence others?

634. How did the term stakeholder originate?

635. Who is the stakeholder?

636. Which stakeholders are thought leaders, influences, or early adopters?

2.31 Risk Management Plan: Serverless Architectures On AWS

637. How risk averse are you?

638. Anticipated volatility of the requirements?

639. How do you manage Serverless Architectures On AWS project Risk?

640. Which risks should get the attention?

641. Do you have a consistent repeatable process that is actually used?

642. Has something like this been done before?

643. Are the participants able to keep up with the workload?

644. What is the impact to the Serverless Architectures On AWS project if the item is not resolved in a timely fashion?

645. Can the risk be avoided by choosing a different alternative?

646. What are it-specific requirements?

647. What can you do to minimize the impact if it does?

648. Do requirements demand the use of new

analysis, design, or testing methods?

649. Are you on schedule?

650. Methodology: how will risk management be performed on this Serverless Architectures On AWS project?

651. For software; does the software interface with new or unproven hardware or unproven vendor products?

652. Risk may be made during which step of risk management?

653. What would you do differently?

654. Havent software Serverless Architectures On AWS projects been late before?

655. Can the Serverless Architectures On AWS project proceed without assuming the risk?

656. Are the reports useful and easy to read?

2.32 Risk Register: Serverless Architectures On AWS

657. Manageability – have mitigations to the risk been identified?

658. When will it happen?

659. When is it going to be done?

660. Are there other alternative controls that could be implemented?

661. Assume the risk event or situation happens, what would the impact be?

662. Who needs to know about this?

663. Why would you develop a risk register?

664. Technology risk -is the Serverless Architectures On AWS project technically feasible?

665. What can be done about it?

666. Do you require further engagement?

667. What is the probability and impact of the risk occurring?

668. Who is going to do it?

669. Have other controls and solutions been

implemented in other services which could be applied as an alternative to additional funding?

670. What should the audit role be in establishing a risk management process?

671. What is your current and future risk profile?

672. What risks might negatively or positively affect achieving the Serverless Architectures On AWS project objectives?

673. What will be done?

674. Are there any gaps in the evidence?

2.33 Probability and Impact Assessment: Serverless Architectures On AWS

675. What is the past performance of the Serverless Architectures On AWS project manager?

676. Do you have specific methods that you use for each phase of the process?

677. What risks does your organization have if the Serverless Architectures On AWS projects fail to meet deadline?

678. Does the customer have a solid idea of what is required?

679. What are the current demands of the customer?

680. Mitigation -how can you avoid the risk?

681. What is the Serverless Architectures On AWS project managers level of commitment and professionalism?

682. Is it necessary to deeply assess all Serverless Architectures On AWS project risks?

683. What are the channels available for distribution to the customer?

684. Are trained personnel, including supervisors and Serverless Architectures On AWS project

managers, available to handle such a large Serverless Architectures On AWS project?

685. Management -what contingency plans do you have if the risk becomes a reality?

686. Does the customer understand the software process?

687. Are enough people available?

688. Do you use diagramming techniques to show cause and effect?

689. Are end-users enthusiastically committed to the Serverless Architectures On AWS project and the system/product to be built?

690. Who should be responsible for the monitoring and tracking of the indicators youhave identified?

691. What are the tools and techniques used in managing the challenges faced?

692. What are its business ethics?

693. Will there be an increase in the political conservatism?

2.34 Probability and Impact Matrix: Serverless Architectures On AWS

694. What is the probability of the risk occurring?

695. How do risks change during the Serverless Architectures On AWS projects life cycle?

696. How do you define a risk?

697. Which phase of the Serverless Architectures On AWS project do you take part in?

698. What will be the impact or consequence if the risk occurs?

699. Are the risk data complete?

700. Is the technology to be built new to your organization?

701. Lay ground work for future returns?

702. How will the consumption pattern change?

703. Is the customer technically sophisticated in the product area?

704. How can you understand and diagnose risks and identify sources?

705. What will be the likely political environment during the life of the Serverless Architectures On AWS

project?

706. Is the customer willing to establish rapid communication links with the developer?

707. If you can not fix it, how do you do it differently?

708. How would you assess the risk management process in the Serverless Architectures On AWS project?

709. How well is the risk understood?

2.35 Risk Data Sheet: Serverless Architectures On AWS

710. What will be the consequences if it happens?

711. What is the environment within which you operate (social trends, economic, community values, broad based participation, national directions etc.)?

712. What will be the consequences if the risk happens?

713. What do people affected think about the need for, and practicality of preventive measures?

714. How reliable is the data source?

715. Whom do you serve (customers)?

716. Will revised controls lead to tolerable risk levels?

717. What are you trying to achieve (Objectives)?

718. What was measured?

719. How do you handle product safely?

720. During work activities could hazards exist?

721. How can hazards be reduced?

722. What are you weak at and therefore need to do better?

723. How can it happen?

724. What can you do?

725. Type of risk identified?

726. What can happen?

727. What were the Causes that contributed?

728. Has a sensitivity analysis been carried out?

729. What are the main threats to your existence?

2.36 Procurement Management Plan: Serverless Architectures On AWS

730. Are vendor invoices audited for accuracy before payment?

731. Have adequate resources been provided by management to ensure Serverless Architectures On AWS project success?

732. Are assumptions being identified, recorded, analyzed, qualified and closed?

733. Are there checklists created to determine if all quality processes are followed?

734. Are action items captured and managed?

735. Are target dates established for each milestone deliverable?

736. Have Serverless Architectures On AWS project management standards and procedures been identified / established and documented?

737. Is there an on-going process in place to monitor Serverless Architectures On AWS project risks?

738. How and when do you enter into Serverless Architectures On AWS project Procurement Management?

739. Are procurement deliverables arriving on time

and to specification?

740. Are Serverless Architectures On AWS project team members committed fulltime?

741. Is Serverless Architectures On AWS project work proceeding in accordance with the original Serverless Architectures On AWS project schedule?

742. What are you trying to accomplish?

743. Are status reports received per the Serverless Architectures On AWS project Plan?

744. Do all stakeholders know how to access the PM repository and where to find the Serverless Architectures On AWS project documentation?

745. What were things that you did very well and want to do the same again on the next Serverless Architectures On AWS project?

746. Is there any form of automated support for Issues Management?

2.37 Source Selection Criteria: Serverless Architectures On AWS

747. Can you identify proposed teaming partners and/ or subcontractors and consider the nature and extent of proposed involvement in satisfying the Serverless Architectures On AWS project requirements?

748. What instructions should be provided regarding oral presentations?

749. Is there collaboration among your evaluators?

750. How should comments received in response to a RFP be handled?

751. When should debriefings be held and how should they be scheduled?

752. What can not be disclosed?

753. Can you reasonably estimate total organization requirements for the coming year?

754. Are considerations anticipated?

755. What are the requirements for publicizing a RFP?

756. With the rapid changes in information technology, will media be readable in five or ten years?

757. How is past performance evaluated?

758. How long will it take for the purchase cost to be the same as the lease cost?

759. What are open book debriefings?

760. Do you prepare an independent cost estimate?

761. What past performance information should be requested?

762. Are responses to considerations adequate?

763. How and when do you enter into Serverless Architectures On AWS project Procurement Management?

764. How do you consolidate reviews and analysis of evaluators?

765. Do you have a plan to document consensus results including disposition of any disagreement by individual evaluators?

766. What procedures are followed when a contractor requires access to classified information or a significant quantity of special material/information?

2.38 Stakeholder Management Plan: Serverless Architectures On AWS

767. Are there checklists created to demine if all quality processes are followed?

768. Does this include subcontracted development?

769. Are post milestone Serverless Architectures On AWS project reviews (PMPR) conducted with your organization at least once a year?

770. Who might be involved in developing a charter?

771. Do any protocols apply for records management?

772. Have reserves been created to address risks?

773. Will the current technology alter during the life of the Serverless Architectures On AWS project?

774. Detail warranty and/or maintenance periods?

775. Is documentation created for communication with the suppliers and vendors?

776. Are there standards for code development?

777. Is pert / critical path or equivalent methodology being used?

778. Are the key elements of a Serverless Architectures On AWS project Charter present?

779. Do all stakeholders know how to access this repository and where to find the Serverless Architectures On AWS project documentation?

780. Have all unresolved risks been documented?

781. Does a documented Serverless Architectures On AWS project organizational policy & plan (i.e. governance model) exist?

782. Are meeting minutes captured and sent out after the meeting?

783. What are reporting requirements?

784. Have you eliminated all duplicative tasks or manual efforts, where appropriate?

2.39 Change Management Plan: Serverless Architectures On AWS

785. What are the responsibilities assigned to each role?

786. What relationships will change?

787. Different application of an existing process?

788. What risks may occur upfront?

789. What is the most positive interpretation it can receive?

790. Do you need new systems?

791. Have the business unit contacts been selected and notified?

792. Identify the current level of skills and knowledge and behaviours of the group that will be impacted on. What prerequisite knowledge do corresponding groups need?

793. How many people are required in each of the roles?

794. What is going to be done differently?

795. Do you need a new organizational structure?

796. What new behaviours are required?

797. Has a training need analysis been carried out?

798. What are the major changes to processes?

799. Has the training provider been established?

800. Who might present the most resistance?

801. What are the needs, priorities and special interests of the audience?

802. Are there any restrictions on who can receive the communications?

803. Are there resource implications for your communications strategy?

804. What skills, education, knowledge, or work experiences should the resources have for each identified competency?

3.0 Executing Process Group: Serverless Architectures On AWS

805. What areas were overlooked on this Serverless Architectures On AWS project?

806. What are the critical steps involved with strategy mapping?

807. Are the necessary foundations in place to ensure the sustainability of the results of the programme?

808. How do you prevent staff are just doing busywork to pass the time?

809. Is the Serverless Architectures On AWS project making progress in helping to achieve the set results?

810. How well did the team follow the chosen processes?

811. What were things that you did very well and want to do the same again on the next Serverless Architectures On AWS project?

812. Who are the Serverless Architectures On AWS project stakeholders?

813. What does it mean to take a systems view of a Serverless Architectures On AWS project?

814. How can software assist in procuring goods and services?

815. Does the Serverless Architectures On AWS project team have the right skills?

816. What were things that you need to improve?

817. Do schedule issues conflicts?

818. What are the critical steps involved in selecting measures and initiatives?

819. What are the Serverless Architectures On AWS project management deliverables of each process group?

820. Does the case present a realistic scenario?

821. Is the schedule for the set products being met?

822. How many different communication channels does the Serverless Architectures On AWS project team have?

3.1 Team Member Status Report: Serverless Architectures On AWS

823. How can you make it practical?

824. Does the product, good, or service already exist within your organization?

825. What specific interest groups do you have in place?

826. How it is to be done?

827. How does this product, good, or service meet the needs of the Serverless Architectures On AWS project and your organization as a whole?

828. How much risk is involved?

829. Will the staff do training or is that done by a third party?

830. Is there evidence that staff is taking a more professional approach toward management of your organizations Serverless Architectures On AWS projects?

831. Do you have an Enterprise Serverless Architectures On AWS project Management Office (EPMO)?

832. When a teams productivity and success depend on collaboration and the efficient flow of information,

what generally fails them?

833. What is to be done?

834. Does every department have to have a Serverless Architectures On AWS project Manager on staff?

835. The problem with Reward & Recognition Programs is that the truly deserving people all too often get left out. How can you make it practical?

836. Are the products of your organizations Serverless Architectures On AWS projects meeting customers objectives?

837. Why is it to be done?

838. How will resource planning be done?

839. Are your organizations Serverless Architectures On AWS projects more successful over time?

840. Are the attitudes of staff regarding Serverless Architectures On AWS project work improving?

841. Does your organization have the means (staff, money, contract, etc.) to produce or to acquire the product, good, or service?

3.2 Change Request: Serverless Architectures On AWS

842. What is a Change Request Form?

843. Has the change been highlighted and documented in the CSCI?

844. Who is included in the change control team?

845. How can you ensure that changes have been made properly?

846. Will this change conflict with other requirements changes (e.g., lead to conflicting operational scenarios)?

847. Change request coordination ?

848. How well do experienced software developers predict software change?

849. Why control change across the life cycle?

850. What should be regulated in a change control operating instruction?

851. What is the relationship between requirements attributes and reliability?

852. Describe how modifications, enhancements, defects and/or deficiencies shall be notified (e.g. Problem Reports, Change Requests etc) and

managed. Detail warranty and/or maintenance periods?

853. Who has responsibility for approving and ranking changes?

854. What type of changes does change control take into account?

855. Has a formal technical review been conducted to assess technical correctness?

856. Who is responsible to authorize changes?

857. Are there requirements attributes that are strongly related to the occurrence of defects and failures?

858. Have all related configuration items been properly updated?

859. What are the requirements for urgent changes?

860. How can changes be graded?

861. What can be filed?

3.3 Change Log: Serverless Architectures On AWS

862. Is the requested change request a result of changes in other Serverless Architectures On AWS project(s)?

863. When was the request approved?

864. Where do changes come from?

865. Is this a mandatory replacement?

866. Does the suggested change request seem to represent a necessary enhancement to the product?

867. How does this relate to the standards developed for specific business processes?

868. Is the submitted change a new change or a modification of a previously approved change?

869. When was the request submitted?

870. Is the change request open, closed or pending?

871. Is the change request within Serverless Architectures On AWS project scope?

872. Is the change backward compatible without limitations?

873. How does this change affect the timeline of the

schedule?

874. How does this change affect scope?

875. Should a more thorough impact analysis be conducted?

876. Who initiated the change request?

877. Will the Serverless Architectures On AWS project fail if the change request is not executed?

878. Do the described changes impact on the integrity or security of the system?

3.4 Decision Log: Serverless Architectures On AWS

879. Does anything need to be adjusted?

880. What eDiscovery problem or issue did your organization set out to fix or make better?

881. Linked to original objective?

882. What is the average size of your matters in an applicable measurement?

883. What alternatives/risks were considered?

884. Do strategies and tactics aimed at less than full control reduce the costs of management or simply shift the cost burden?

885. How does an increasing emphasis on cost containment influence the strategies and tactics used?

886. What was the rationale for the decision?

887. What is the line where eDiscovery ends and document review begins?

888. With whom was the decision shared or considered?

889. Which variables make a critical difference?

890. It becomes critical to track and periodically revisit both operational effectiveness; Are you noticing all that you need to, and are you interpreting what you see effectively?

891. Is everything working as expected?

892. How consolidated and comprehensive a story can you tell by capturing currently available incident data in a central location and through a log of key decisions during an incident?

893. Behaviors; what are guidelines that the team has identified that will assist them with getting the most out of team meetings?

894. Adversarial environment. is your opponent open to a non-traditional workflow, or will it likely challenge anything you do?

895. How effective is maintaining the log at facilitating organizational learning?

896. Meeting purpose; why does this team meet?

897. Decision-making process; how will the team make decisions?

898. What are the cost implications?

3.5 Quality Audit: Serverless Architectures On AWS

899. How does your organization know that the range and quality of its accommodation, catering and transportation services are appropriately effective and constructive?

900. How does your organization know that its staff embody the core knowledge, skills and characteristics for which it wishes to be recognized?

901. How does your organization know that it is appropriately effective and constructive in preparing its staff for organizational aspirations?

902. What review processes are in place for your organizations major activities?

903. How does your organization know that its Governance system is appropriately effective and constructive?

904. Are storage areas and reconditioning operations designed to prevent mix-ups and assure orderly handling of both the distressed and reconditioned devices?

905. How does your organization know that its system for commercializing research outputs is appropriately effective and constructive?

906. How does your organization know that its

teaching activities (and staff learning) are effectively and constructively enhanced by its activities?

907. How does your organization know that the quality of its supervisors is appropriately effective and constructive?

908. How does your organization know that its relationships with other relevant organizations are appropriately effective and constructive?

909. Are all areas associated with the storage and reconditioning of devices clean, free of rubbish, adequately ventilated and in good repair?

910. How does your organization know that its research funding systems are appropriately effective and constructive in enabling quality research outcomes?

911. How does your organization know that its staff are presenting original work, and properly acknowledging the work of others?

912. How does your organization know that its staff entrance standards are appropriately effective and constructive and being implemented consistently?

913. How does your organization know that its system for inducting new staff to maximize workplace contributions are appropriately effective and constructive?

914. What mechanisms exist for identification of staff development needs?

915. How does your organization know that its system for examining work done is appropriately effective and constructive?

916. Has a written procedure been established to identify devices during all stages of receipt, reconditioning, distribution and installation so that mix-ups are prevented?

917. How does your organization know that its relationships with the community at large are appropriately effective and constructive?

918. How does your organization know that its public relations and marketing systems are appropriately effective and constructive?

3.6 Team Directory: Serverless Architectures On AWS

919. Who will report Serverless Architectures On AWS project status to all stakeholders?

920. Where should the information be distributed?

921. How does the team resolve conflicts and ensure tasks are completed?

922. Process decisions: which organizational elements and which individuals will be assigned management functions?

923. How will you accomplish and manage the objectives?

924. Timing: when do the effects of communication take place?

925. Who are the Team Members?

926. What are you going to deliver or accomplish?

927. Process decisions: are there any statutory or regulatory issues relevant to the timely execution of work?

928. Process decisions: is work progressing on schedule and per contract requirements?

929. Why is the work necessary?

930. How will the team handle changes?

931. What needs to be communicated?

932. Who will write the meeting minutes and distribute?

933. Process decisions: how well was task order work performed?

934. Process decisions: are all start-up, turn over and close out requirements of the contract satisfied?

935. Process decisions: do job conditions warrant additional actions to collect job information and document on-site activity?

936. Have you decided when to celebrate the Serverless Architectures On AWS projects completion date?

937. When does information need to be distributed?

3.7 Team Operating Agreement: Serverless Architectures On AWS

938. Why does your organization want to participate in teaming?

939. How do you want to be thought of and known within your organization?

940. What is culture?

941. How will you resolve conflict efficiently and respectfully?

942. Did you recap the meeting purpose, time, and expectations?

943. What is group supervision?

944. How will you divide work equitably?

945. Do you record meetings for the already stated unable to attend?

946. Methodologies: how will key team processes be implemented, such as training, research, work deliverable production, review and approval processes, knowledge management, and meeting procedures?

947. Do you solicit member feedback about meetings and what would make them better?

948. Communication protocols: how will the team communicate?

949. Do you ask participants to close laptops and place mobile devices on silent on the table while the meeting is in progress?

950. Confidentiality: how will confidential information be handled?

951. What are some potential sources of conflict among team members?

952. What are the boundaries (organizational or geographic) within which you operate?

953. Conflict resolution: how will disputes and other conflicts be mediated or resolved?

954. What is a Virtual Team?

955. Do you vary your voice pace, tone and pitch to engage participants and gain involvement?

956. What types of accommodations will be formulated and put in place for sustaining the team?

957. Do you leverage technology engagement tools group chat, polls, screen sharing, etc.?

3.8 Team Performance Assessment: Serverless Architectures On AWS

958. When a reviewer complains about method variance, what is the essence of the complaint?

959. To what degree will the approach capitalize on and enhance the skills of all team members in a manner that takes into consideration other demands on members of the team?

960. Social categorization and intergroup behaviour: Does minimal intergroup discrimination make social identity more positive?

961. To what degree does the teams work approach provide opportunity for members to engage in results-based evaluation?

962. Does more radicalness mean more perceived benefits?

963. To what degree do members articulate the goals beyond the team membership?

964. To what degree does the team possess adequate membership to achieve its ends?

965. Can team performance be reliably measured in simulator and live exercises using the same assessment tool?

966. To what degree do team members articulate the

teams work approach?

967. Which situations call for a more extreme type of adaptiveness in which team members actually re-define roles?

968. To what degree will the team ensure that all members equitably share the work essential to the success of the team?

969. To what degree do the goals specify concrete team work products?

970. Where to from here?

971. To what degree does the teams work approach provide opportunity for members to engage in open interaction?

972. To what degree are the goals realistic?

973. If you have received criticism from reviewers that your work suffered from method variance, what was the circumstance?

974. To what degree will the team adopt a concrete, clearly understood, and agreed-upon approach that will result in achievement of the teams goals?

975. What are you doing specifically to develop the leaders around you?

976. How does Serverless Architectures On AWS project termination impact Serverless Architectures On AWS project team members?

977. Do friends perform better than acquaintances?

3.9 Team Member Performance Assessment: Serverless Architectures On AWS

978. How do you make use of research?

979. How was the determination made for which training platforms would be used (i.e., media selection)?

980. What is the role of the Reviewer?

981. What steps have you taken to improve performance?

982. What qualities does a successful Team leader possess?

983. What is a significant fact or event?

984. What are the basic principles and objectives of performance measurement and assessment?

985. To what degree does the teams approach to its work allow for modification and improvement over time?

986. In what areas would you like to concentrate your knowledge and resources?

987. How do you currently account for your results in the teams achievement?

988. To what degree are the goals ambitious?

989. Should a ratee get a copy of all the raters documents about the employees performance?

990. What are the staffs preferences for training on technology-based platforms?

991. To what degree are sub-teams possible or necessary?

992. Is it clear how goals will be accomplished?

993. To what degree do team members frequently explore the teams purpose and its implications?

994. How is performance assessment used in making future award decisions including options and extend/compete decisions?

995. What are top priorities?

3.10 Issue Log: Serverless Architectures On AWS

996. Do you prepare stakeholder engagement plans?

997. Why multiple evaluators?

998. What help do you and your team need from the stakeholders?

999. How do you reply to this question; you am new here and managing this major program. How do you suggest you build your network?

1000. Who do you turn to if you have questions?

1001. Where do team members get information?

1002. What approaches to you feel are the best ones to use?

1003. Is the issue log kept in a safe place?

1004. Why do you manage human resources?

1005. How often do you engage with stakeholders?

1006. Can you think of other people who might have concerns or interests?

1007. Is access to the Issue Log controlled?

1008. Why do you manage communications?

1009. What steps can you take for positive relationships?

1010. What are the stakeholders interrelationships?

1011. Who needs to know and how much?

1012. What are the typical contents?

4.0 Monitoring and Controlling Process Group: Serverless Architectures On AWS

1013. How was the program set-up initiated?

1014. Is the program in place as intended?

1015. Did it work?

1016. How can you monitor progress?

1017. Is the program making progress in helping to achieve the set results?

1018. How well did the chosen processes produce the expected results?

1019. Contingency planning. if a risk event occurs, what will you do?

1020. Key stakeholders to work with. How many potential communications channels exist on the Serverless Architectures On AWS project?

1021. What input will you be required to provide the Serverless Architectures On AWS project team?

1022. Were decisions made in a timely manner?

1023. What good practices or successful experiences or transferable examples have been identified?

1024. How well did the chosen processes fit the needs of the Serverless Architectures On AWS project?

1025. Did you implement the program as designed?

1026. How many potential communications channels exist on the Serverless Architectures On AWS project?

1027. If a risk event occurs, what will you do?

1028. What is the expected monetary value of the Serverless Architectures On AWS project?

1029. What resources (both financial and non-financial) are available/needed?

1030. How is agile program management done?

4.1 Project Performance Report: Serverless Architectures On AWS

1031. To what degree are the members clear on what they are individually responsible for and what they are jointly responsible for?

1032. To what degree does the task meet individual needs?

1033. To what degree do team members feel that the purpose of the team is important, if not exciting?

1034. What is the degree to which rules govern information exchange between groups?

1035. To what degree can the cognitive capacity of individuals accommodate the flow of information?

1036. To what degree does the teams purpose contain themes that are particularly meaningful and memorable?

1037. Next Steps?

1038. To what degree do team members agree with the goals, relative importance, and the ways in which achievement will be measured?

1039. To what degree does the information network communicate information relevant to the task?

1040. To what degree is the team cognizant of small

wins to be celebrated along the way?

1041. To what degree does the funding match the requirement?

1042. To what degree do team members understand one anothers roles and skills?

1043. To what degree can the team ensure that all members are individually and jointly accountable for the teams purpose, goals, approach, and work-products?

1044. To what degree does the teams purpose constitute a broader, deeper aspiration than just accomplishing short-term goals?

1045. To what degree can all members engage in open and interactive considerations?

1046. To what degree are the tasks requirements reflected in the flow and storage of information?

1047. To what degree can the team measure progress against specific goals?

1048. To what degree is there a sense that only the team can succeed?

4.2 Variance Analysis: Serverless Architectures On AWS

1049. Does the contractors system provide unit or lot costs when applicable?

1050. Why do variances exist?

1051. Do work packages consist of discrete tasks which are adequately described?

1052. How does your organization measure performance?

1053. What is the dollar amount of the fluctuation?

1054. What can be the cause of an increase in costs?

1055. How have the setting and use of standards changed over time?

1056. Contract line items and end items?

1057. Do you identify potential or actual budget-based and time-based schedule variances?

1058. Are authorized changes being incorporated in a timely manner?

1059. Is work progressively subdivided into detailed work packages as requirements are defined?

1060. Did an existing competitor change strategy?

1061. Are all budgets assigned to control accounts?

1062. Are indirect costs accumulated for comparison with the corresponding budgets?

1063. The anticipated business volume?

1064. What is your organizations rationale for sharing expenses and services between business segments?

1065. Is all contract work included in the CWBS?

1066. Are indirect costs charged to the appropriate indirect pools and incurring organization?

1067. Are overhead costs budgets established on a basis consistent with the anticipated direct business base?

1068. How does your organization allocate the cost of shared expenses and services?

4.3 Earned Value Status: Serverless Architectures On AWS

1069. Earned value can be used in almost any Serverless Architectures On AWS project situation and in almost any Serverless Architectures On AWS project environment. it may be used on large Serverless Architectures On AWS projects, medium sized Serverless Architectures On AWS projects, tiny Serverless Architectures On AWS projects (in cut-down form), complex and simple Serverless Architectures On AWS projects and in any market sector. some people, of course, know all about earned value, they have used it for years - but perhaps not as effectively as they could have?

1070. Where is evidence-based earned value in your organization reported?

1071. Validation is a process of ensuring that the developed system will actually achieve the stakeholders desired outcomes; Are you building the right product? What do you validate?

1072. If earned value management (EVM) is so good in determining the true status of a Serverless Architectures On AWS project and Serverless Architectures On AWS project its completion, why is it that hardly any one uses it in information systems related Serverless Architectures On AWS projects?

1073. Verification is a process of ensuring that the developed system satisfies the stakeholders agreements and specifications; Are you building the product right? What do you verify?

1074. How much is it going to cost by the finish?

1075. Are you hitting your Serverless Architectures On AWS projects targets?

1076. When is it going to finish?

1077. Where are your problem areas?

1078. What is the unit of forecast value?

1079. How does this compare with other Serverless Architectures On AWS projects?

4.4 Risk Audit: Serverless Architectures On AWS

1080. What compliance systems do you have in place to address quality, errors, and outcomes?

1081. Are formal technical reviews part of this process?

1082. What are the legal implications of not identifying a complete universe of business risks?

1083. Does your organization have a process for meeting its ongoing taxation obligations?

1084. Is the auditor able to evaluate contradictory evidence in an unbiased manner?

1085. Are Serverless Architectures On AWS project requirements stable?

1086. Has risk management been considered when planning an event?

1087. How do you manage risk?

1088. Does the adoption of a business risk audit approach change internal control documentation and testing practices?

1089. Are procedures developed to respond to foreseeable emergencies and communicated to all involved?

1090. Does willful intent modify risk-based auditing?

1091. Is the auditor truly independent?

1092. What are the boundaries of the auditors responsibility for policing management fidelity?

1093. Is the customer willing to participate in reviews?

1094. Does the implementation method matter?

1095. Do you have an understanding of insurance claims processes?

1096. What can you do to manage outcomes?

1097. Is all expenditure authorised through an identified process?

1098. Extending the consideration on the halo effect, to what extent are auditors able to build skepticism in evidence review?

1099. For paid staff, does your organization comply with the minimum conditions for employment and/or the applicable modern award?

4.5 Contractor Status Report: Serverless Architectures On AWS

1100. What is the average response time for answering a support call?

1101. What was the overall budget or estimated cost?

1102. What was the final actual cost?

1103. Are there contractual transfer concerns?

1104. If applicable; describe your standard schedule for new software version releases. Are new software version releases included in the standard maintenance plan?

1105. What are the minimum and optimal bandwidth requirements for the proposed solution?

1106. What was the actual budget or estimated cost for your organizations services?

1107. Describe how often regular updates are made to the proposed solution. Are corresponding regular updates included in the standard maintenance plan?

1108. What was the budget or estimated cost for your organizations services?

1109. Who can list a Serverless Architectures On AWS project as organization experience, your organization or a previous employee of your organization?

1110. What process manages the contracts?

1111. How is risk transferred?

1112. How does the proposed individual meet each requirement?

1113. How long have you been using the services?

4.6 Formal Acceptance: Serverless Architectures On AWS

1114. How does your team plan to obtain formal acceptance on your Serverless Architectures On AWS project?

1115. Did the Serverless Architectures On AWS project manager and team act in a professional and ethical manner?

1116. Was the sponsor/customer satisfied?

1117. What can you do better next time?

1118. Was business value realized?

1119. Does it do what Serverless Architectures On AWS project team said it would?

1120. Was the Serverless Architectures On AWS project work done on time, within budget, and according to specification?

1121. Was the Serverless Architectures On AWS project managed well?

1122. How well did the team follow the methodology?

1123. Do you buy-in installation services?

1124. Does it do what client said it would?

1125. General estimate of the costs and times to complete the Serverless Architectures On AWS project?

1126. What function(s) does it fill or meet?

1127. Was the client satisfied with the Serverless Architectures On AWS project results?

1128. Did the Serverless Architectures On AWS project achieve its MOV?

1129. What are the requirements against which to test, Who will execute?

1130. Do you perform formal acceptance or burn-in tests?

1131. Who supplies data?

1132. What is the Acceptance Management Process?

1133. Have all comments been addressed?

5.0 Closing Process Group: Serverless Architectures On AWS

1134. Mitigate. what will you do to minimize the impact should a risk event occur?

1135. What were the desired outcomes?

1136. What will you do to minimize the impact should a risk event occur?

1137. What is the Serverless Architectures On AWS project name and date of completion?

1138. Is there a clear cause and effect between the activity and the lesson learned?

1139. What could have been improved?

1140. Did the Serverless Architectures On AWS project team have the right skills?

1141. Does the close educate others to improve performance?

1142. Were risks identified and mitigated?

1143. What were things that you did very well and want to do the same again on the next Serverless Architectures On AWS project?

1144. What do you need to do?

1145. Did the Serverless Architectures On AWS project management methodology work?

1146. Was the user/client satisfied with the end product?

1147. Who are the Serverless Architectures On AWS project stakeholders?

1148. Were escalated issues resolved promptly?

1149. Based on your Serverless Architectures On AWS project communication management plan, what worked well?

1150. Is this a follow-on to a previous Serverless Architectures On AWS project?

1151. What areas were overlooked on this Serverless Architectures On AWS project?

5.1 Procurement Audit: Serverless Architectures On AWS

1152. Are transportation charges verified?

1153. Does the individual having check-signing responsibility review the use of the signature plates?

1154. Where required, did candidates give evidence of complying with required environmental management standards?

1155. How do you address the risk of fraud and corruption?

1156. Does your organization have an overall strategy and/or policy on public procurement, providing guidance for procuring entities?

1157. What are the required standards of quality assurance or environmental management?

1158. Were calculations used in evaluation adequate and correct?

1159. Does the procurement function/unit have the ability to apply public procurement principles and to prepare tender and contract documents?

1160. Does the strategy ensure that appropriate controls are in place to ensure propriety and regularity in delivery?

1161. Are the rules for automatic payment in computer programs approved by management prior to implementation?

1162. Is the opportunity properly published?

1163. Were the performance conditions under the contract comprehensive and unambiguous?

1164. Are there performance targets on value for money obtained and cost savings?

1165. Are all pre-numbered checks accounted for on a regular basis?

1166. Is there no evidence that the expert has influenced the decisions taken by the public authority in his/her interest or in the interest of a specific contractor?

1167. Was the dynamic purchasing system set up following the rules of open procedure?

1168. Did the conditions included in the contract protect the risk of non-performance by the supplier and were there no conflicting provisions?

1169. Are there procedures governing the negotiations of long-term contracts?

1170. Is trend analysis performed on expenditures made by key employees and by vendor?

1171. Was a sufficient competitive environment created?

5.2 Contract Close-Out: Serverless Architectures On AWS

1172. Was the contract complete without requiring numerous changes and revisions?

1173. Have all contracts been completed?

1174. Has each contract been audited to verify acceptance and delivery?

1175. Change in circumstances?

1176. Have all contracts been closed?

1177. Was the contract type appropriate?

1178. Change in attitude or behavior?

1179. Are the signers the authorized officials?

1180. Have all acceptance criteria been met prior to final payment to contractors?

1181. Have all contract records been included in the Serverless Architectures On AWS project archives?

1182. Change in knowledge?

1183. How/when used ?

1184. Parties: who is involved?

1185. What happens to the recipient of services?

1186. How is the contracting office notified of the automatic contract close-out?

1187. How does it work?

1188. What is capture management?

1189. Was the contract sufficiently clear so as not to result in numerous disputes and misunderstandings?

1190. Parties: Authorized?

5.3 Project or Phase Close-Out: Serverless Architectures On AWS

1191. What were the goals and objectives of the communications strategy for the Serverless Architectures On AWS project?

1192. Can the lesson learned be replicated?

1193. What was expected from each stakeholder?

1194. What are they?

1195. What information is each stakeholder group interested in?

1196. Did the Serverless Architectures On AWS project management methodology work?

1197. In addition to assessing whether the Serverless Architectures On AWS project was successful, it is equally critical to analyze why it was or was not fully successful. Are you including this?

1198. Who controlled key decisions that were made?

1199. How often did each stakeholder need an update?

1200. What is in it for you?

1201. What stakeholder group needs, expectations, and interests are being met by the Serverless

Architectures On AWS project?

1202. Did the delivered product meet the specified requirements and goals of the Serverless Architectures On AWS project?

1203. What was the preferred delivery mechanism?

1204. What information did each stakeholder need to contribute to the Serverless Architectures On AWS projects success?

1205. If you were the Serverless Architectures On AWS project sponsor, how would you determine which Serverless Architectures On AWS project team(s) and/or individuals deserve recognition?

1206. Who exerted influence that has positively affected or negatively impacted the Serverless Architectures On AWS project?

1207. Were messages directly related to the release strategy or phases of the Serverless Architectures On AWS project?

1208. Planned remaining costs?

5.4 Lessons Learned: Serverless Architectures On AWS

1209. What is the skill mix defined for the staffing?

1210. What were the problems encountered in the Serverless Architectures On AWS project-functional area relationship, why, and how could they be fixed?

1211. Would you spend your own money to fix this issue?

1212. Who needs to learn lessons?

1213. Were any strategies or activities unsuccessful?

1214. How actively and meaningfully were stakeholders involved in the Serverless Architectures On AWS project?

1215. Why does your organization need a lessons learned (LL) capability?

1216. What is your working hypothesis, if you have one?

1217. Whom to share Lessons Learned Information with?

1218. What report generation capability is needed?

1219. What was the single greatest success and the single greatest shortcoming or challenge from the Serverless Architectures On AWS projects perspective?

1220. How often do communications get lost?

1221. Who had fiscal authority to manage the funding for the Serverless Architectures On AWS project, did that work?

1222. Was the change control process properly implemented to manage changes to cost, scope, schedule, or quality?

1223. How complete and timely were the materials you were provided to decide whether to proceed from one Serverless Architectures On AWS project lifecycle phase to the next?

1224. Were the aims and objectives achieved?

1225. What were the main sources of frustration in the Serverless Architectures On AWS project?

1226. How was the Serverless Architectures On AWS project controlled?

1227. How useful was your testing?

1228. How useful was the format and content of the Serverless Architectures On AWS project Status Report to you?

Index

satisfying 101, 215
savings 25, 43, 60, 262
scales 79
scaling 93, 98, 103, 112, 114, 125
scenario 26, 222
scenarios 225
schedule 3-4, 28, 64, 119, 148, 159, 161, 170, 179-182, 187,
199, 204, 214, 222, 228, 234, 249, 255, 268
scheduled 147, 195, 215
schedules 153, 179-180
scheduling 161-162, 181
scheme 85, 119
science 51
Scorecard 2, 12-14
scorecards 78
Scores 14
scoring 10
screen 237
second 12, 72
section 12, 23, 36, 49, 61, 76, 90, 131
sector 251
secure 68, 97, 107, 127
securing 92-93
security 21, 63, 67, 79-80, 83, 93, 96, 104, 113, 115, 129-
130, 137, 156, 228
segmented 33
segments 30, 106, 250
select 40, 48, 54, 67, 73, 86, 95
selected 68, 71, 185-186, 219
selecting 222
selection 5, 116, 215, 241
self-host 121
seller 175, 183
sellers 1
selling 111
senior 82, 101, 113, 189
sensitive 42, 52, 55, 141
sequence 163, 169
sequencing 141, 199
series 11
seriously 138
server 18, 95, 98-99, 103, 111-112, 114, 116, 127

CPSIA information can be obtained
at www.ICGtesting.com
Printed in the USA
BVHW081014130819
555775BV00018B/940/P